Campaign Rules

Campaign Rules

A 50-State Guide to Campaigns and Elections in America

Nina Kasniunas and Daniel M. Shea

ROWMAN & LITTLEFIELD PUBLISHERS, INC.
Lanham • Boulder • New York • Toronto • Plymouth, UK

Published by Rowman & Littlefield Publishers, Inc.
A wholly owned subsidary of The Rowman & Littlefield Publishing Group, Inc.
4501 Forbes Boulevard, Suite 200, Lanham, Maryland 20706
http://www.rowmanlittlefield.com

Estover Road, Plymouth PL6 7PY, United Kingdom

British Library Cataloguing in Publication Information Available

Library of Congress Cataloging-in-Publication Data
Kasniunas, Nina, 1971–
   Campaign rules : a 50-state guide to campaigns and elections in America / Nina Kasniunas and Daniel M. Shea.
      p. cm.
   Includes index.
   ISBN 978-1-4422-0175-0 (cloth : alk. paper) — ISBN 978-1-4422-0177-4 (electronic)
   1. Election law—United States—States. 2. Campaign funds—Law and legislation—United States—States. I. Shea, Daniel M. II. Title.
   KF4886.K37 2010
   342.73'07—dc22   2009043117

Printed in the United States of America

CONTENTS

INTRODUCTION

Most Americans believe the surest way to change public policy is to change the personnel of the government. If you do not like what government is doing, simply bring to power a set of leaders who share your concerns and are determined to act accordingly. This "public reflection" process seems to be the heart of the democratic system. Open, competitive elections pit candidates with different ideas about the proper role of government against each other. These candidates battle it out on an equal playing field, working to attract as many followers as possible and, in the end average citizens decide which individuals should get a shot at governing.

Elections seem the perfect mechanism to merge three core American beliefs: egalitarianism, which implies that all people are created equal and all have a right to participate in the conduct of government; populism, which means average folks have a great deal of wisdom (and conversely, that there is much to fear about elites); and majority will. Indeed, Americans place such faith in elections that enfranchisement is often viewed as the panacea to the problems confronted by groups in society. As noted by a prominent student of elections:

> The established American response to social discontent is the extension of the ballot. The protests of women led to their enfranchisement, but not to the end of sexual discrimination. Antiwar sentiments of the young facilitated the enfranchisement of eighteen-year-olds, even as fighting continued in Vietnam. Black discontent was answered by passage of voting rights laws, but not by any fundamental economic legislation. Elections themselves are seen as the basic solution for social problems.[1]

It is not surprising, then, that elections, both for candidates and increasingly to decide policy questions, are used heavily in America. Some would suggest we are the most election-crazed nation in the world, boasting roughly 500,000 elected positions nationwide. We elect a president and members of the national legislature, of course, but also governors, thousands of state legislators, county officials, mayors and city officials, town trustees, judicial officers, sheriffs and other law enforcement officials, assessors, attorney generals, comptrollers, auditors, and people to scores of other government posts. In some communities the choice of animal control officer (i.e., dog catchers) is put to a ballot.

Not only do we rely heavily on elections to fill government positions, but the frequency of these events far outpaces what is found in other nations. Some Americans focus on elections every four years, given that this is when we select a president, but elections are held in every community every year. State and federal legislators are selected every two years, and most municipal posts are filled during the odd-numbered years. Moreover, given that party organizations now nominate candidates to run in the general election through separate primary elections, it is fair to say that Americans are called to the polls no less than twice every year—once for the primary and once for the general election.

Americans use elections not only to select candidates, but to directly change government policy as well. Referendums and ballot initiatives allow average citizens to vote on policy matters, essentially sidestepping the legislative process. In some states, voters may even remove elected officials from office in a special election; this is called recall. Polling data suggests that interest in these sorts of opportunities is growing. Many believe this process is an even more perfect reflection of the public will than candidate-centered elections, but others are quick to point out numerous down sides.

While there has always been a good deal of interest in electoral politics, one could reasonably argue that the focus in this area has heightened since the 2008 election. Indeed, there is mounting evidence to suggest the number of Americans voting and volunteering in the recent contest set a 50-year high. Today most Americans view electoral politics as a viable avenue for change.

This surge of interest in elections is reflected in the growing number of college offerings in the area and in related topics. And the class sizes are growing; as young Americans rediscover the power of electoral politics, they flock to classes that will help them better understand the process. We might also point to the growing number of graduate and undergraduate programs in applied politics. Whereas a few years ago only a handful existed, today there are at least a dozen such programs.

The presidential contest grabbed the attention of the nation, but most realize that state and local elections are critically important, and that an individual's efforts at this level could have a dramatic impact. Instructors of college offerings in parties and elections, as well as introductory course in American Government, often push their students to become involved in state and local campaigns, realizing that the likelihood of their playing a meaningful role is greater.

Indeed, one of the most curious, and in many ways telling, aspects of the Constitution is the delegation of election rules and qualifications to the states. Article I, section 4 of the Constitutions notes that the "times, places, and manner of holding elections" is to be "prescribed in each state by the legislature thereof." Congress, nevertheless, is given the opportunity to change these laws as they see fit. The intent was to allow states to regulate the election process, so long as the Congress remained silent.

In order to help secure state ratification of the Constitution, the Federalists offered to add a list of amendments designed to protect citizens from acts by the government, which of course became the first ten amendments, or the Bill of Rights. Nowhere in this list of individual protections is a right to participate in elections. Given the wording and intent of the original Constitution, and the absence of any protections as amendments, the opportunity for Congress to restrict voting was left open. Simply put, while elections were considered the centerpiece of the *state* political process, for the new federal government they were less central.

The outcome has been that, for the most part, the rules and regulations guiding elections vary from state-to-state. Some states allow voters to vote early, others do not. Some states grant citizens "same day" registration; others impose as much as a 30-day parameter. Mail in balloting is allowed in some states, but not others. Some states allow ballot initiatives, others do not. And the complexity of state campaign finance regulations is staggering.

This volume is designed to provide students, researchers, and activists an array of state-based electoral information. It is designed as a "quick reference" tool to help sort out the dizzying breadth of electoral rules. One of the challenges of constructing a book of this sort—what some would say a significant danger—is that state election rules, regulations, and dates are continually changing. While we are confident that the material in the pages to follow was accurate and up-to-date when the book was published, we ask that the reader also recognize the fluid nature of "campaign rules."

NOTE

1. Gerald M. Pomper, *Elections in America: Control and Influence in Democratic Politics*, 2nd ed. (New York: Longman, 1980), 3.

ALABAMA

STATE VOTER TURNOUT

Population: 4,599,030
Registered Voters
    2000: 2,528,963
    2002: 2,327,974
    2004: 2,597,629
    2006: 2,469,807
    2008: 2,693,758
Turnout
    2000: 50.1% (Highest Office/Voting-Age Pop.): 1,672,551 / 3,334,714
    2002: 40.4% (Highest Office/Voting-Age Pop.): 1,364,602 / 3,365,217
    2004: 55.2% (Highest Office/Voting-Age Pop.): 1,883,415 / 3,410,003
    2006: 35.9% (Highest Office/Voting-Age Pop.): 1,250,401 / 3,481,823
    2008: 59.1% (Highest Office/Voting-Age Pop.): 2,099,819 / 3,551,926
Youth Turnout (18–29 years old)
    2000: 45%
    2002: 27%
    2004: 44%
    2006: 26%
    2008: 53%

STATEWIDE ELECTION OUTCOMES

Presidential Vote 2004: 1,883,449 votes cast
    Bush (R)   62.5%
    Kerry (D)   36.8%
Presidential Vote 2008: 2,099,819 votes cast
    Obama (D)   38.7%
    McCain (R)   60.3%
Gubernatorial Vote 2006: 1,250,401 votes cast
    Riley (R)   57.4%
    Baxley (D)   41.6%
Electoral College Votes: 9

VOTING REGULATIONS

Residency Requirements: Alabama resident for at least one day.
Absentee Ballot: Yes
    Criteria: Available for individuals unable to be at voting booth on election days for acceptable reasons, including: absence from county,

illness or disability, military service, college, election officer at polling place other than his/her own and working a required shift during polling hours. Applications must be received by 5th calendar day prior to election. Ballot must be received by day prior to election.

Advance Voting: No
Provisional Balloting: Yes
Vote by Phone: No
Registration Deadline: 10 days prior to election
Secretary of State Website: http://www.sos.state.al.us/Default.aspx

CANDIDATE REGULATIONS

Qualifications
Governor: 30 years old, state resident for 7 years, U.S. citizen for 10 years
State Senator: 25 years old, district resident for 1 year, state resident for 3 years, U.S. citizen for 1 day
State Representative: 21 years old, district resident for 1 year, state resident for 3 years, U.S. citizen for 1 day

Filing Fees
Governor
Independents: $0
Democrats: $1,430 (2% of base salary)
Republicans: $1,430 (2% of base salary)

State Senate
Independents: $0
Democrats: $600 (set to change for 2010) deadline beginning of April 2010
Republicans: $500 (set to change for 2010) deadline end of April 2010

State House
Independents: $0
Democrats: $600 (set to change for 2010) deadline beginning of April 2010
Republicans: $500 (set to change for 2010) deadline end of April 2010

Filing Deadlines
Presidential Primary: November 7
Independent/Third Party in Presidential Election: September 6
Congressional Primary: April 2, 2010
Independent/Third Party in General Election: June 1, 2010
Online Filing: No

Petition Signature Requirements
　　Major Party: President: 37,513 (3% of qualified electors in last general election for governor)
　　Minor Party: President: 5,000 signatures (qualified electors; valid addresses must appear)

JUDICIAL ELECTIONS

Justice Chosen: At large
Method of Selection
　　Unexpired Term: Gubernatorial appointment
　　Full Term: Partisan election
No. of Judges: 9
Terms: 6 years
Method of Retention: Partisan election

PRIMARY ELECTION PROCESS

Presidential
　　Type: Primary/Open
　　Date: February 5, 2008
State
　　Type: Primary/Open
　　Date: June 1, 2010

STATE CAMPAIGN FINANCE

Contribution Regulations: Corporations are limited to $500 per candidate, political committee, or political party per election. Private individuals, political parties, labor unions, political action committees, or other political committee may contribute unlimited amounts to candidates or committees.
Fundraising Limits: Candidates are not limited to the amount they are allowed to raise.
Online Filing: No
Reporting Cycle Dates: Candidates must file reports 50–45 days before and 10–5 days before the primary election; 10–5 days before the primary run-off; and 50–45 days before and 10–5 days before the general election. An annual report must also be filled in January, no later than January 31.

LOBBYING GUIDELINES

All lobbyists are required to register and file quarterly reports no later than January 31, April 30, July 31, or October 31 with the Alabama Ethics Commission.

BALLOT INITIATIVES AND REFERENDUM

Referendum: No
Ballot Initiative: No
Recall Election: No

Alaska

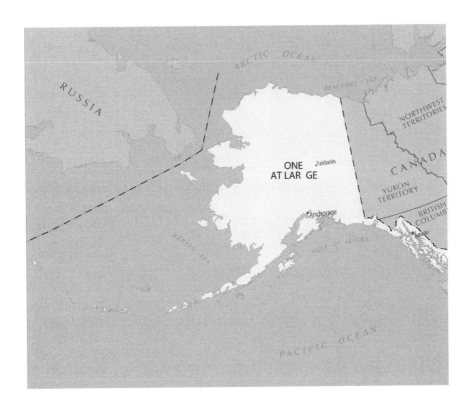

STATE VOTER TURNOUT

Population: 670,053
Registered Voters
  2000: 473,648
  2002: 460,855
  2004: 472,160
  2006: 466,258
  2008: 490,656
Turnout
  2000: 65% (Highest Office/Voting-Age Pop.): 285,560 / 439,782
  2002: 51% (Highest Office/Voting-Age Pop.): 231,484 / 458,143
  2004: 65.2% (Highest Office/Voting-Age Pop.): 312,598 / 479,579
  2006: 47.8% (Highest Office/Voting-Age Pop.): 237,322 / 496,387
  2008: 63.7% (Highest Office/Voting-Age Pop.): 323,820 / 508,136
Youth Turnout (18–29 years old)
  2000: 52%
  2002: 34%
  2004: 58%
  2006: 30%
  2008: 49%

STATEWIDE ELECTION OUTCOMES

Presidential Vote 2004: 312,598 votes cast
  Bush (R)   61.1%
  Kerry (D)   35.5%
Presidential Vote 2008: 323,820 votes cast
  Obama (D)   37.8%
  McCain (R) 59.5%
Gubernatorial Vote 2006: 237,322 votes cast
  Palin (R)   48.3%
  Knowles (D) 41.0%
Electoral College Votes: 3

VOTING REGULATIONS

Residency Requirements: Resident of Alaska and election district for 30 days
Absentee Ballot: Yes
  Criteria: Available for voters unable to be at voting booth on election days. Application must be received at least 10 days prior to election.

Advance Voting: Yes
    Criteria: Available for voters qualifying for absentee ballot. Early in-person absentee voting is available beginning 15 days before election.
Provisional Balloting: Yes
Vote by Phone: No
Registration Deadline: 30 days prior to election
Secretary of State Website: http://www.elections.alaska.gov/

CANDIDATE REGULATIONS

Qualifications
    Governor: 30 years old, state resident for 7 years, U.S. citizen for 7 years
    State Senator: 25 years old, district resident for 1 year, state resident for 7 years
    State Representative: 21 years old, district resident for 1 year, state resident for 7 years
Filing Fees
    Governor: $100
    State Senate: $30
    State House: $30
Filing Deadlines
    Presidential Primary: n/a (Presidential Caucus on February 5)
    Independent/Third Party in Presidential Election: August 6
    Congressional Primary: June 1, 2010
    Independent/Third Party in General Election: June 1, 2010
Online Filing: No
Petition Signature Requirements:
    Major Party: President: 7,124 (Registered Voters; 3% of total votes in last general election)
    Minor Party: President: 3,128 (1% of total votes in last general election)

JUDICIAL ELECTIONS

Justice Chosen: At large
Method of Selection
    Unexpired Term: Gubernatorial appointment from judicial nominating commission.
    Full Term: Gubernatorial appointment from judicial nominating commission.
No. of Judges: 5
Terms: 10 years
Method of Retention: Retention Election: no expired judicial terms

PRIMARY ELECTION PROCESS

Presidential
　　Type: Caucus/Closed
　　Date: February 5, 2008
State
　　Type: Caucus/Closed
　　Date: August 24, 2010

STATE CAMPAIGN FINANCE

Contribution Regulations: Individuals are limited to $500 per year to a candidate or group that is not a political party. To political parties, individuals are limited to $5,000. Groups that are not political parties are limited to $1,000 per year to candidates, other groups, or parties. Loans are included in these contribution limits whether or not they are repaid. Political parties are limited to $100,000 per year to a committee for Governor/Lieutenant Governor candidate, $15,000 per year to a committee for a State Senate candidate, $10,000 per year to a committee for a State House candidate, $5,000 per year to a committee for a candidate to a constitutional convention, a committee for a judge seeking retention, or a committee for a candidate for municipal office. There are no limits for self-funding candidates, with specific amounts unable to be recovered for each office. Corporations are prohibited from making campaign contributions. Individuals and groups are not limited in the contributions given to a ballot proposition or question.
Fundraising Limits: Candidates are not limited to the amount they are allowed to raise.
Online Filing: Yes
Reporting Cycle Dates: Candidates (not in exempt counties) must file campaign disclosure reports 30 days before the election and on February 15 for those expenditures and contributions not reported in the prior year. Individuals, municipalities, groups, or ongoing organizations may also be asked to disclose a report under certain circumstances.

LOBBYING GUIDELINES

All lobbyists are required to register and file reports on February 10, April 25, and July 10 with the Alaska Public Offices Commission.

BALLOT INITIATIVES AND REFERENDUM

Referendum: Yes
Ballot Initiative: Yes
Recall Election: Yes

ARIZONA

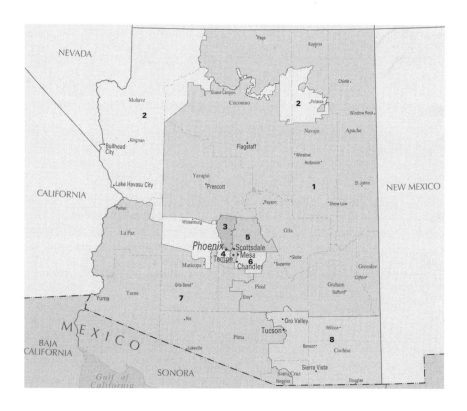

STATE VOTER TURNOUT

Population: 6,166,318
Registered Voters
  2000: 2,173,122
  2002: 2,216,435
  2004: 2,642,120
  2006: 2,568,401
  2008: 2,987,451
Turnout
  2000: 40.2% (Highest Office/Voting-Age Pop.): 1,532,016 / 3,826,035
  2002: 30.7% (Highest Office/Voting-Age Pop): 1,226,111 / 4,035,058
  2004: 47.0% (Highest Office/Voting-Age Pop.): 2,012,585 / 4,279,620
  2006: 33.3% (Highest Office/Voting-Age Pop.): 1,526,782 / 4,582,842
  2008: 47.4% (Highest Office/Voting-Age Pop.): 2,293,475 / 4,834,316
Youth Turnout (18–29 years old)
  2000: 29%
  2002: 11%
  2004: 42%
  2006: 23%
  2008: 47%

STATEWIDE ELECTION OUTCOMES

Presidential Vote 2004: 2,012,585 votes cast
  Bush (R)   54.9%
  Kerry (D)   44.4%
Presidential Vote 2008: 2,293,475 votes cast
  Obama (D)   45.1%
  McCain (R)   53.6%
Gubernatorial Vote 2006: 1,533,645 votes cast
  Napolitano (D) 62.6%
  Munsil (R)   35.4%
Electoral College Votes: 10

VOTING REGULATIONS

Residency Requirements: Arizona resident
Absentee Ballot: Yes
  Criteria: No excuse is necessary for an absentee ballot; request for a regular early ballot must be received by 7:00 p.m. on day of election.

Advance Voting: Yes
  Criteria: Begins 33 days before election, ends at 5:00 p.m. on Friday before election.
Provisional Balloting: Yes
Vote by Phone: No
Registration Deadline: October 10, 2010 at midnight
Secretary of State Website: http://www.azsos.gov/election/

CANDIDATE REGULATIONS

Qualifications
  Governor: 25 years old, state resident for 5 years, U.S. citizen for 10 years
  State Senator: 25 years old, county resident for 1 year, state resident for 3 years
  State Representative: 25 years old, county resident for 1 year, state resident for 3 years
Filing Fees
  Governor: $0
  State Senate: $0
  State House: $0
Filing Deadlines
  Presidential Primary: December 17, 5:00 p.m.
  Independent/Third Party in Presidential Election: June 4, 5:00 p.m.
  Congressional Primary: May 26, 2010
  Independent/Third Party in General Election: May 26, 2010
Online Filing: No
Petition Signature Requirements
  Major Party: 20,449 (One-half of 1%/no more than 10% of registered voters of the candidates party)
  Minor Party: President: 21,759 (One-half of 1% of registered voters by county)

JUDICIAL ELECTIONS

Justice Chosen: At large
Method of Selection
  Unexpired Term: Gubernatorial appointment from judicial nominating commission.
  Full Term: Gubernatorial appointment from judicial nominating commission.

No. of Judges: 5
Terms: 6 years
Method of Retention: Retention Election

PRIMARY ELECTIONS

Presidential
  Type: Primary/Closed
  Date: February 5, 2008
State
  Type: Primary/Closed
  Date: August 31, 2010

STATE CAMPAIGN FINANCE

Contribution Regulations: Individuals are limited to $840 per year to a candidate or group that is not a political party. To political parties, individuals are limited to $5,850. Candidates during the primary stage of the election may receive no more than $83,448 from all political committees and parties combined unless they win the nomination, in which case they may receive more contributions that again will be limited to no more than $83,448 for the general election. State also has a system of public financing for candidates under the Clean Election program. See http://www.ccec .state.az.us/ccecweb/ccecays/home.asp for details on this program.
Fundraising Limits: Candidates may not accept more than $83,448 for a statewide office worth of contributions, $8,352 for non-statewide local candidates, and $10,440 for non-statewide legislative candidates.
Online Filing: Yes
Reporting Cycle Dates: All candidates who raise or spend more than $500 must designate a campaign committee within 10 days. All standing campaign committees must file a statement with the Secretary of State each year.

LOBBYING GUIDELINES

All lobbyists are required to register with the Arizona Secretary of State and pay a registration fee of $25. Quarterly reports are to be done, the first to be by March 1, and may be filed electronically.

BALLOT INITIATIVES AND REFERENDUM

Referendum: Yes
Ballot Initiative: Yes
Recall Election: Yes

ARKANSAS

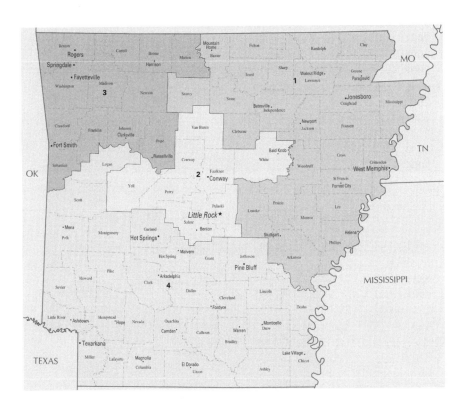

STATE VOTER TURNOUT

Population: 2,810,872
Registered Voters
  2000: 1,555,809
  2002: 1,455,882
  2004: 1,699,934
  2006: 1,615,271
  2008: 1,641,542
Turnout
  2000: 46.0% (Highest Office/Voting-Age Pop.): 921,781 / 2,002,370
  2002: 39.7% (Highest Office/Voting-Age Pop.): 805,696 / 2,031,067
  2004: 51.0% (Highest Office/Voting-Age Pop.): 1,054,945 / 2,069,151
  2006: 35.4% (Highest Office/Voting-Age Pop.): 749,991 / 2,120,139
  2008: 49.5% (Highest Office/Voting-Age Pop.): 1,068,963 / 2,159,125
Youth Turnout (18–29 years old)
  2000: 41%
  2002: 21%
  2004: 40%
  2006: 21%
  2008: 35%

STATEWIDE ELECTION OUTCOMES

Presidential Vote 2004: 1,054,945 votes cast
  Bush (R)   54.3%
  Kerry (D)   44.6%
Presidential Vote 2008: 1,068,963 votes cast
  Obama (D)   38.8%
  McCain (R)   58.8%
Gubernatorial Vote 2006: 774,680 votes cast
  Beebe (D)   55.6%
  Hutchinson(R)   40.7%
Electoral College Votes: 6

VOTING REGULATIONS

Residency Requirements: Arkansas resident for at least one day
Absentee Ballot: Yes
  Criteria: Available for voters who are unavoidably absent from polling
  place on day of election; unable to attend polling place due to illness or

injury; members of U.S. military; or temporarily living outside of territorial United States. Ballot must be returned by close of business on day before election.

Advance Voting: Yes

    Criteria: Available for all voters 15 days prior to election.

Provisional Balloting: Yes

Vote by Phone: No

Registration Deadline: 30 days prior to election

Secretary of State Website: http://www.sosweb.state.ar.us/elections.html

CANDIDATE REGULATIONS

Qualifications

    Governor: 30 years old, state resident for 7 years

    State Senator: 25 years old, district resident for 1 year, state resident for 2 years

    State Representative: 21 years old, district resident for 1 year, state resident for 2 years

Filing Fees

    Governor

        Independents: $0

        Democrats: Party will set fees for next election in January 2010

        Republicans: Party will set fees for next election in January 2010

    State Senate

        Independents: $0

        Democrats: Party will set fees for next election in January 2010

        Republicans: Party will set fees for next election in January 2010

    State House

        Independents: $0

        Democrats: To be determined

        Republicans: State GOP will set fees for next election in January 2010

Filing Deadlines

    Presidential Primary: November 7

    Independent/Third Party in Presidential Election: September 6

    Congressional Primary: March 8, 2010, 12:00 p.m.

    Independent/Third Party in General Election: May 1, 2010, 12:00 p.m.

Online Filing: No

Petition Signature Requirements

    Major Party: President: 10,000 signatures

    Minor Party: President: 1,000 signatures

JUDICIAL ELECTIONS

Justice Chosen: At large
Method of Selection
  Unexpired Term: Gubernatorial appointment
  Full Term: Nonpartisan election
No. of Judges: 7
Terms: 8 years
Method of Retention: Nonpartisan election

PRIMARY ELECTION PROCESS

Presidential
  Type: Primary/Open
  Date: February 5, 2008
State
  Type: Primary/Open
  Date: May 23, 2010

STATE CAMPAIGN FINANCE

Contribution Regulations: Individuals are limited to contributions of $1,000 per candidate per election. Political parties are limited to $2,500 per candidate per election. Cash contributions must be under $100 and anonymous contributions must be under $50.
Fundraising Limits: Candidates are not limited to the amount they are allowed to raise; however, expenditures over $50 must not be made in cash.
Online Filing: No
Reporting Cycle Dates: Candidates are required to file quarterly reports of contributions and expenditures.

LOBBYING GUIDELINES

All lobbyists must register within 5 days of beginning. Within 15 days of the end of a quarter, each lobbyist must file a report with the Secretary of State. These reports are open to the public.

BALLOT INITIATIVES AND REFERENDUM

Referendum: Yes
Ballot Initiative: Yes
Recall Election: No

CALIFORNIA

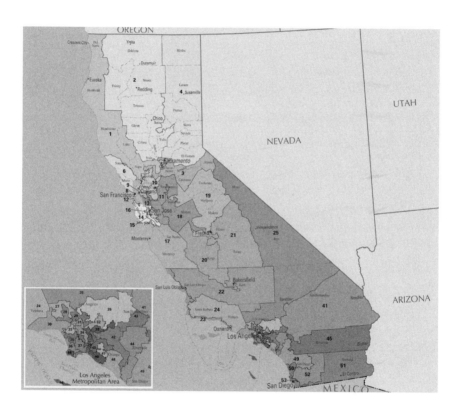

STATE VOTER TURNOUT

Population: 36,457,549
Registered Voters
   2000: 15,707,307
   2002: 15,173,112
   2004: 16,646,555
   2006: 15,837,108
   2008: 16,171,772
Turnout
   2000: 44.1% (Highest Office/Voting-Age Pop.): 10,965,849 / 24,892,775
   2002: 29.0% (Highest Office/Voting-Age Pop.): 7,476,351 / 25,719,077
   2004: 47.1% (Highest Office/Voting-Age Pop.): 12,421,852 / 26,380,324
   2006: 23.2% (Highest Office/Voting-Age Pop.): 8,679,416 / 26,955,438
   2008: 49.4% (Highest Office/Voting-Age Pop.): 13,561,900 / 27,466,418
Youth Turnout (18–29 years old)
   2000: 40%
   2002: 22%
   2004: 46%
   2006: 25%
   2008: 53%

STATEWIDE ELECTION OUTCOMES

Presidential Vote 2004: 12,421,353 votes cast
   Bush (R)   44.4%
   Kerry (D)   54.3%
Presidential Vote 2008: 13,561,900 votes cast
   Obama (D)   61.1%
   McCain (R)   37.0%
Gubernatorial Vote 2006: 8,679,416 votes cast
   Schwarzenegger (R) 55.9%
   Angelides (D)   38.9%
Electoral College Votes: 55

VOTING REGULATIONS

Residency Requirements: California resident for at least one day
Absentee Ballot: Yes
   Criteria: Ballot may be requested until 7 days prior to election and returned by 8:00 p.m. on day of election.

Advance Voting: Available for all voters. Times vary by county.
Provisional Balloting: Yes
Vote by Phone: No
Registration Deadline: 15 days prior to election
Secretary of State Website: http://www.sos.ca.gov/elections/elections.htm

CANDIDATE REGULATIONS

Qualifications
  Governor: 18 years old, state resident, and U.S. citizen for 5 years
  State Senator: 18 years old, district resident for 1 year, U.S. citizen for 3 years
  State Representative: 18 years old, district resident for 1 year, U.S. citizen for 3 years
Filing Fees
  Governor: $3,500 (equal to 2% of first year's salary)
  State Senate: $1,162.08 (equal to 1% of first year's salary)
  State House: $1,162.08 (equal to 1% of first year's salary)
Filing Deadlines
  Presidential Primary: December 4 (Democrats), November 23 (other parties)
  Independent/Third Party in Presidential Election: August 8
  Congressional Primary: March 12, 2010
  Independent/Third Party in General Election: August 6, 2010
Online Filing: No
Petition Signature Requirements:
  Major Party: President: 88,991 (Registered Voters; 1% of registered voters for the party.)
  Minor Party: President: 158,372 (1% of registered voters from the last federal general election.)

JUDICIAL ELECTIONS

Justice Chosen: At large
Method of Selection
  Unexpired Term: Gubernatorial appointment
  Full Term: Gubernatorial appointment
No. of Judges: 7
Terms: 12 years
Method of Retention: Retention election

PRIMARY ELECTION PROCESS

Presidential
   Type: Primary/Democrats: Semiclosed; Republicans: Closed
   Date: February 5, 2008
State
   Type: Primary/Democrats: Semiclosed; Republicans: Closed
   Date: June 8, 2010

STATE CAMPAIGN FINANCE

Contribution Regulations: Individual contributions are regulated only in special elections when local limitations are in place; however, the state has also created "small contributor committees," which have special status. These committees receive contributions from 100 or more people, with each person contributing no more than $200, and makes contributions to 5 or more candidates. Contributions from sources other than these small contributor committees are limited to $20,000 for gubernatorial races, $5,000 for other statewide elective elections, and $3,000 for other elective office. Candidates are limited to $100,000 to contribute to their own campaign. Cash and anonymous contributions must be less than $100.
Fundraising Limits: Expenditures over $100 may not be made in cash. There are voluntary spending limits for candidates, which allow them to purchase special space in a state ballot pamphlet. These limits are $6 million in primary elections, $10 million in general elections for gubernatorial candidates; $4 million in primary elections and $6 million in general statewide elections other than for governor or the State Board of Equalization; $1 million in primary elections and $1.5 million in general elections for a candidate for the State Board of Equalization; $600,000 in primary elections and $900,000 in general elections for candidate for State Senate; $400,000 in primary elections and $700,000 in general elections for candidate for the Assembly.
Online Filing: Yes
Reporting Cycle Dates: Candidates are required to file quarterly reports of contributions and expenditures.

LOBBYING GUIDELINES

All lobbyists must register with the Secretary of State within 10 days of beginning, pay a fee of no more than $25, and file periodic reports.

BALLOT INITIATIVES AND REFERENDUM

Referendum: Yes
Ballot Initiative: Yes
Recall Election: Yes

Colorado

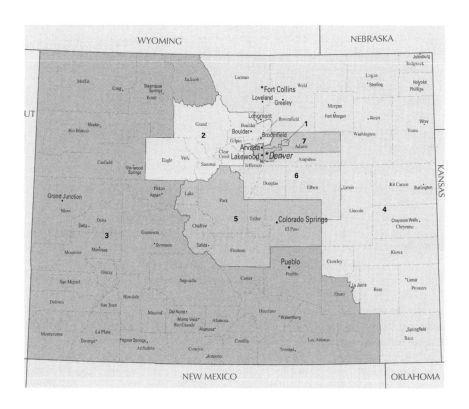

STATE VOTER TURNOUT

Population: 4,753,377
Registered Voters
  2000: 2,274,152
  2002: 2,247,944
  2004: 3,101,956
  2006: 3,000,836
  2008: 3,203,583
Turnout
  2000: 53.7% (Highest Office/Voting-Age Pop.): 1,741,368 / 3,250,040
  2002: 42.0% (Highest Office/Voting-Age Pop.): 1,416,093 / 3,381,530
  2004: 61.2% (Highest Office/Voting-Age Pop.): 2,129,630 / 3,479,710
  2006: 43.1% (Highest Office/Voting-Age Pop.): 1,558,405 / 3,617,942
  2008: 64.0% (Highest Office/Voting-Age Pop.): 2,401,361 / 3,753,483
Youth Turnout (18–29 years old)
  2000: 37%
  2002: 29%
  2004: 50%
  2006: 31%
  2008: 52%

STATEWIDE ELECTION OUTCOMES

Presidential Vote 2004: 2,147,224 votes cast
  Bush (R)   51.3%
  Kerry (D)   46.7%
Presidential Vote 2008: 2,401,361 votes cast
  Obama (D)   53.7%
  McCain (R)   44.7%
Gubernatorial Vote 2006: 1,558,387 votes cast
  Ritter (D)   57.0%
  Beauprez (R) 40.2%
Electoral College Votes: 9

VOTING REGULATIONS

Residency Requirements: Colorado resident at present address for 30 days
Absentee Ballot: Yes

Criteria: Application must be received 7 days before election; ballot must be returned by 7:00 p.m. on day of election.

Advance Voting: Yes

Criteria: Available to all voters 10 days before primary elections and 15 days before general election.

Provisional Balloting: Yes

Vote by Phone: No

Registration Deadline: 29 days prior to election

Secretary of State Website: http://www.elections.colorado.gov/DDefault.aspx?tid=984

CANDIDATE REGULATIONS

Qualifications

Governor: 30 years old, state resident for 2 years

State Senator: 25 years old, district resident for 1 year

State Representative: 25 years old, district resident for 1 year

Filing Fees

Governor: $0

Independents: none

Democrats: none

Republicans: none

State Senate: $0

Independents: none

Democrats: none

Republicans: none

State House: $0

Independents: none

Democrats: none

Republicans: none

Filing Deadlines

Presidential Primary: November 7

Independent/Third Party in Presidential Election: September 6

Congressional Primary: May 27, 2010

Independent/Third Party in General Election: May 27, 2010 (Third Party), June 15, 2010 (Independent)

Online Filing: No

Petition Signature Requirements

Major Party: President: 1,000 (registered voters)

Minor Party: President: Pay $50 fee

JUDICIAL ELECTIONS

Justice Chosen: At large
Method of Selection
  Unexpired Term: Gubernatorial appointment from judicial nominating commission.
  Full Term: Gubernatorial appointment from judicial nominating commission.
No. of Judges: 7
Terms: 10 years
Method of Retention: Retention election

PRIMARY ELECTION PROCESS

Presidential
  Type: Caucus/Closed
  Date: February 5, 2008
State
  Type: Caucus/Closed
  Date: August 10, 2010

STATE CAMPAIGN FINANCE

Contribution Regulations: Contributions more than $100 cannot be made in cash. Political parties are limited to contributions of $10,000 for candidates for the House of Representatives, State Board of Education, or regent of the University of Colorado; $15,000 for State Senate; $20,000 for Lieutenant Governor; $80,000 for Secretary of State, Attorney General, or State Treasurer; $400,000 for Governor. Individuals are limited to contributions of $25,000 per year to political parties.
Fundraising Limits: Candidates are not limited to the amount they are allowed to raise.
State Offices: State offices are required to follow the state campaign laws as stated above.
Online Filing: Yes
Reporting Cycle Dates: Candidates must report quarterly in off-election years (April 15, July 15, October 15, and January 15) and on the 1st day of each month beginning the 6th full month before the election, 14 days before, and 30 days after the major election in election years.

LOBBYING GUIDELINES

All lobbyists must register with the Secretary of State within 10 days of beginning, pay a fee of $25 for electronic file and $50 otherwise, and file monthly reports.

BALLOT INITIATIVES AND REFERENDUM

Referendum: Yes
Ballot Initiative: Yes
Recall Election: Yes

CONNECTICUT

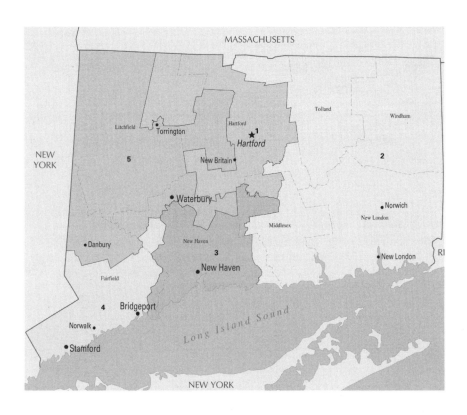

STATE VOTER TURNOUT

Population: 3,405,565
Registered Voters
 2000: 1,874,245
 2002: 1,847,247
 2004: 1,831,567
 2006: 1,941,467
 2008: 2,104,989
Turnout
 2000: 56.6% (Highest Office/Voting-Age Pop.): 1,459,525 / 2,575,724
 2002: 38.9% (Highest Office/Voting-Age Pop.): 1,022,942 / 2,614,622
 2004: 59.7% (Highest Office/Voting-Age Pop.): 1,578,769 / 2,645,063
 2006: 42.5% (Highest Office/Voting-Age Pop.): 1,134,780 / 2,673,154
 2008: 78.2% (Highest Office/Voting-Age Pop.): 1,646,797 / 2,104,989
Youth Turnout (18–29 years old)
 2000: 45%
 2002: 23%
 2004: 44%
 2006: 22%
 2008: 52%

STATEWIDE ELECTION OUTCOMES

Presidential Vote 2004: 1,578,757 votes cast
 Bush (R)   43.9%
 Kerry (D)   54.3%
Presidential Vote 2008: 1,646,797 votes cast
 Obama (D)   60.6%
 McCain (R)   38.2%
Gubernatorial Vote 2006: 1,123,412 votes cast
 Rell (R)   63.2%
 DeStefano (D)   35.4%
Electoral College Votes: 7

VOTING REGULATIONS

Residency Requirements: Connecticut resident for at least one day.
Absentee Ballot: Yes
 Criteria: Ballot must be returned by close of polls on day of election.
Advance Voting: No

Provisional Balloting: Yes
Vote by Phone: Yes
Registration Deadline: 14 days prior to election by mail; 7 days prior to election in person.
Secretary of State Website: http://www.sots.ct.gov/sots/cwp/view.asp?a=3&q=415810

CANDIDATE REGULATIONS

Qualifications
  Governor: 30 years old, state resident
  State Senator: 21 years old, district resident
  State Representative: 21 years old, district resident
Filing Fees
  Governor: $0
    Independents: $0
    Democrats: $0
    Republicans: $0
  State Senate: $0
    Independents: $0
    Democrats: $0
    Republicans: $0
  State House: $0
    Independents: $0
    Democrats: $0
    Republicans: $0
Filing Deadlines
  Presidential Primary: November 7
  Independent/Third Party in Presidential Election: September 6
  Congressional Primary: May 25, 2010
  Independent/Third Party in General Election: August 4, 2010
Online Filing: No
Petition Signature Requirements
  Major Party: President: No requirement
  Minor Party: President: 7,500 signatures

JUDICIAL ELECTIONS

Justice Chosen: At large
Method of Selection
  Unexpired Term: Gubernatorial appointment from judicial nominating commission with consent of the legislature.

Full Term: Gubernatorial appointment from judicial nominating commission with consent of the legislature.

No. of Judges: 7

Terms: 8 years

Method of Retention: Gubernatorial appointment from judicial nominating commission with consent of the legislature.

PRIMARY ELECTION PROCESS

Presidential
   Type: Primary/Closed
   Date: February 5, 2008
State
   Type: Primary/Closed
   Date: August 10, 2010

STATE CAMPAIGN FINANCE

Contribution Regulations: Individuals are limited to aggregate contributions of $15,000 per election—$2,500 for Governor; $1,500 for Lieutenant Governor, Secretary of State, Treasurer, Controller, or Attorney General; $1,000 for chief executive of a town, city, or borough; $500 for State Senator or Probate Judge; $250 for State Representative or other municipal office. Corporate and labor organization contributions are prohibited, but labor political action committees may contribute up to $50,000 per election—denominations concurrent with those of individual regulations. Cash contributions are limited to $50. Anonymous contributions are limited to $15. All contributions more than $100 must be made by personal check. Contributions by persons less than 15 years of age are limited to $30.

Fundraising Limits: Candidates are not limited to the amount they are allowed to raise.

Online Filing: Yes, if contributions or expenditures are over $250,000 reports must be filed electronically and in hard copy.

Reporting Cycle Dates: January 11, 2010, further dates are yet to be determined

LOBBYING GUIDELINES

All lobbyists are required to register biannually and file quarterly reports between the 1st and 10th of the months of April, July, and January.

BALLOT INITIATIVES AND REFERENDUM

Referendum: No
Ballot Initiative: No
Recall Election: No

Delaware

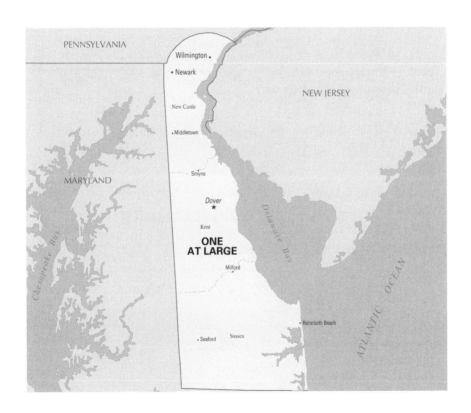

STATE VOTER TURNOUT

Population: 864,764
Registered Voters
  2000: 505,360
  2002: 618,000
  2004: 553,917
  2006: 557,736
  2008: 588,052
Turnout
  2000: 54.9% (Highest Office/Voting-Age Pop.): 327,529 / 594,138
  2002: 37.9% (Highest Office/Voting-Age Pop.): 232,314 / 611,288
  2004: 59.4% (Highest Office/Voting-Age Pop.): 375,190 / 631,509
  2006: 39.0% (Highest Office/Voting-Age Pop.): 254,099 / 652,189
  2008: 68.7% (Highest Office/Voting-Age Pop.): 413,562 / 602,317
Youth Turnout (18–29 years old)
  2000: 45%
  2002: 23%
  2004: 44%
  2006: 22%
  2008: 54%

STATEWIDE ELECTION OUTCOMES

Presidential Vote 2004: 374,836 votes cast
  Bush (R)   45.8%
  Kerry (D)   53.3%
Presidential Vote 2008: 412,412 votes cast
  Obama (D)   58.8%
  McCain (R)   36.9%
Gubernatorial Vote 2008: 395,204 votes cast
  Markell (D)   67.5%
  Lee (R)   32.0%
Electoral College Votes: 3

VOTING REGULATIONS

Residency Requirements: Delaware resident for at least one day.
Absentee Ballot: Yes
  Criteria: Available for voters affirming that they are unable to reach polling place during election.

Advance Voting: No
　Criteria: Available as absentee voting in person; available polling hours vary by district.
Provisional Balloting: Yes
Vote by Phone: No
Registration Deadline: 20 days prior to election (Deadline extended to 3rd Monday before election for overseas citizens and military members)
Secretary of State Website: http://elections.delaware.gov/

CANDIDATE REGULATIONS

Qualifications
　Governor: 30 years old, state resident for 6 years, U.S. citizen for 12 years
　State Senator: 27 years old, jurisdiction resident for 1 year, state resident for 3 years
　State Representative: 24 years old, jurisdiction resident for 1 year, state resident for 3 years
Filing Fees
　Governor: $5,300 (2010 fees will be determined in February 2010)
　State Senate: $1,590 (2010 fees will be determined in February 2010)
　State House: $795 (2010 fees will be determined in February 2010)
Filing Deadlines
　Presidential Primary: December 10
　Independent/Third Party in Presidential Election: July 25 (Independent), September 1 (Third Party)
　Congressional Primary: July 30, 2010
　Independent/Third Party in General Election: September 1, 2010
Online Filing: No
Petition Signature Requirements
　Major Party: President: 284 signatures (Registered Voters)
　Minor Party: President: 5,678 signatures

JUDICIAL ELECTIONS

Justice Chosen: At large
Method of Selection
　Unexpired Term: Gubernatorial appointment from judicial nominating commission with consent of the legislature.
　Full Term: Gubernatorial appointment from judicial nominating commission with consent of the legislature.

No. of Judges: 5
Terms: 12 years
Method of Retention: Gubernatorial appointment from judicial nominating commission with consent of the legislature.

PRIMARY ELECTION PROCESS

Presidential
  Type: Primary/Closed
  Date: February 5, 2008
State
  Type: Primary/Closed
  Date: September 14, 2010

STATE CAMPAIGN FINANCE

Contribution Regulations: Individuals are limited to $20,000 for political parties, $1,200 for statewide candidates, and $600 for non-statewide candidates. Contributions in cash are limited to $50 and anonymous contributions are prohibited.
Fundraising Limits: Candidates are limited to $75,000 for gubernatorial elections; $25,000 for statewide offices and NCC executives; $15,000 for NCC President; $5,000 for all other country offices and state senate; $3,000 for state house of representatives and all other offices.
Online Filing: No
Reporting Cycle Dates: All candidates are required to file reports with the State Election Commissioner for each reporting period. Details are available on the State Election Commissioner website.

LOBBYING GUIDELINES

All lobbyists are required to register and file quarterly reports with the State Public Inquiry Commission.

BALLOT INITIATIVES AND REFERENDUM

Referendum: No
Ballot Initiative: No
Recall Election: No

FLORIDA

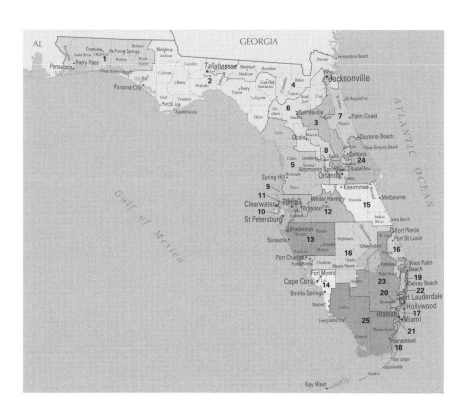

STATE VOTER TURNOUT

Population: 18,251,243
Registered Voters
  2000: 8,752,717
  2002: 9,334,814
  2004: 10,300,942
  2006: 10,433,148
  2008: 11,247,634
Turnout
  2000: 47.9% (Highest Office/Voting-Age Pop.): 5,963,110 / 12,473,796
  2002: 39.5% (Highest Office/Voting-Age Pop.): 5,100,581 / 12,973,336
  2004: 56.1% (Highest Office/Voting-Age Pop.): 7,609,810 / 13,553,481
  2006: 34.3% (Highest Office/Voting-Age Pop.): 4,829,270 / 14,085,749
  2008: 74.6% (Highest Office/Voting-Age Pop.): 8,390,744 / 11,247,634
Youth Turnout (18–29 years old)
  2000: 40%
  2002: 23%
  2004: 49%
  2006: 18%
  2008: 53%

STATEWIDE ELECTION OUTCOMES

Presidential Vote 2004: 1,883,449 votes cast
  Bush (R)   62.5%
  Kerry (D)   36.8%
Presidential Vote 2008: 8,390,744 votes cast
  Obama (D)   51.0%
  McCain (R)   48.2%
Gubernatorial Vote 2006: 4,829,270 votes cast
  Crist (R)   52.2%
  Davis (D)   45.1%
Electoral College Votes: 27

VOTING REGULATIONS

Residency Requirements: Florida resident for at least one day.
Absentee Ballot: Yes
  Criteria: Available for all voters. Must be requested 5 days before election; must be returned by 7:00 p.m. on day of election.

Advance Voting: Yes
   Criteria: Begins 15 days before election
Provisional Balloting: Yes
Vote by Phone: No
Registration Deadline: October 4, 2010
Secretary of State Website: http://election.dos.state.fl.us/

CANDIDATE REGULATIONS

Qualifications
   Governor: 30 years old, state resident for 7 years
   State Senator: 21 years old, district resident, state resident for 2 years
   State Representative: 21 years old, district resident, state resident for 2 years
Filing Fees
   Governor: 6% of annual salary ($7,743.60 as of 2006)
   State Senate: $1,915.92 (partisan), $1,277.28 (no party affiliation)
   State House: $1,915.92 (partisan), $1,277.28 (no party affiliation)
Filing Deadlines
   Presidential Primary: October 31
   Independent/Third Party in Presidential Election: July 15
   Congressional Primary: April 30, 2010
   Independent/Third Party in General Election: March 29, 2010, 12:00 p.m.
Online Filing: No
Petition Signature Requirements
   Major Party: President: No requirement
   Minor Party: President: 104,334 (1% of total registered voters)

JUDICIAL ELECTIONS

Justice Chosen: Regional
Method of Selection
   Unexpired Term: Gubernatorial appointment from judicial nominating commission.
   Full Term: Gubernatorial appointment from judicial nominating commission.
No. of Judges: 7
Terms: 6 years
Method of Retention: Retention election

PRIMARY ELECTION PROCESS

Presidential:
   Type: Primary/Closed
   Date: January 29, 2008
State
   Type: Primary/Closed
   Date: August 24, 2010

STATE CAMPAIGN FINANCE

Contribution Regulations: Contributions may not be solicited or accepted during the 60-day period of regular legislative session. Cash contributions are limited to $100. Individuals and political committees other than political parties are limited to contributions of $500 to any candidate. Candidates for the offices of Governor and Lieutenant Governor are considered to be a single candidate for the purposes of the contribution limitations. Unemancipated children under the age of 18 are limited to contributions of $100.
Fundraising Limits: Candidates are limited to $50,000 from national, state, or county political party executive committee. No more than $25,000 can be received in a 28-day period prior to the election.
Online Filing: No
Reporting Cycle Dates: Committees of continuous existence must file reports with the Division of Elections annually each January. Candidates and political committees must file regular quarterly reports by the tenth day following the end of the quarter, on the 4th, 18th, and 32nd days immediately before the 1st and 2nd primaries, and on the 4th and 18th days immediately before the general election.

LOBBYING GUIDELINES

All lobbyists are required to register annually and submit reports biannually to the Lobbyist Registration Office.

BALLOT INITIATIVES AND REFERENDUM

Referendum: No
Ballot Initiative: Yes
Recall Election: No

GEORGIA

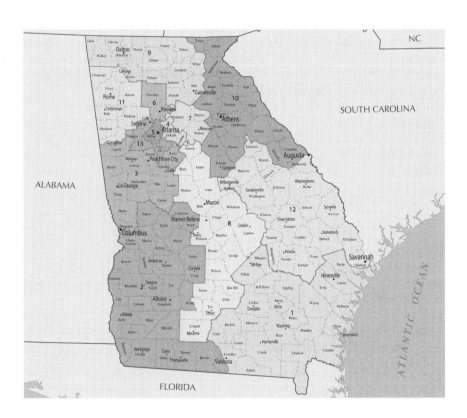

STATE VOTER TURNOUT

Population: 9,363,941
Registered Voters
  2000: 3,859,960
  2002: 3,758,178
  2004: 4,248,802
  2006: 4,408,840
  2008: 5,598,425
Turnout
  2000: 42.4% (Highest Office/Voting-Age Pop.): 2,583,208 / 6,099,347
  2002: 32.2% (Highest Office/Voting-Age Pop.): 2,031,604 / 6,352,186
  2004: 50.0% (Highest Office/Voting-Age Pop.): 3,301,875 / 6,606,838
  2006: 30.7% (Highest Office/Voting-Age Pop.): 2,122,258 / 6,915,512
  2008: 70.1% (Highest Office/Voting-Age Pop.): 3,924,486 / 5,598,425
Youth Turnout (18–29 years old)
  2000: 40%
  2002: 22%
  2004: 49%
  2006: 29%
  2008: 51%

STATEWIDE ELECTION OUTCOMES

Presidential Vote 2004: 3,298,798 votes cast
  Bush (R)   58.0%
  Kerry (D)   41.4%
Presidential Vote 2008: 3,924,486 votes cast
  Obama (D)   47.0%
  McCain (R) 52.2%
Gubernatorial Vote 2006: 2,122,185 votes cast
  Perdue (R)   57.9%
  Taylor (D)   38.2%
Electoral College Votes: 15

VOTING REGULATIONS

Residency Requirements: Georgia resident for at least one day.
Absentee Ballot: Yes
  Criteria: No reason is required. May be requested up to 180 days before
election; must be received by 7:00 p.m. on day of election.

Advance Voting: Yes
　Criteria: Available Monday through Friday of week prior to election.
Provisional Balloting: Yes
Vote by Phone: No
Registration Deadline: 30 days prior to election.
Secretary of State Website: http://sos.georgia.gov/elections/

CANDIDATE REGULATIONS

Qualifications
　Governor: 30 years old, state resident for 6 years, U.S. citizen for 15 years
　State Senator: 25 years old, district resident for 1 year, state resident for 2 years
　State Representative: 21 years old, district resident for 1 year, state resident for 2 years
Filing Fees
　Governor: $3,867.09
　State Senate: $400
　State House: $400
Filing Deadlines
　Presidential Primary: November 1
　Independent/Third Party in Presidential Election: July 15
　Congressional Primary: April 30, 2010
　Independent/Third Party in General Election: July 13, 2010
Online Filing: No
Petition Signature Requirements
　Major Party: President: 44,089 signatures
　Minor Party: President: 42,489 signatures

JUDICIAL ELECTIONS

Justice Chosen: At large
Method of Selection
　Unexpired Term: Gubernatorial appointment from judicial nominating commission.
　Full Term: Nonpartisan election
No. of Judges: 7
Terms: 6 years
Method of Retention: Nonpartisan election

PRIMARY ELECTION PROCESS

Presidential
  Type: Primary/Open
  Date: February 5, 2008
State
  Type: Primary/Open
  Date: July 20, 2010

STATE CAMPAIGN FINANCE

Contribution Regulations: Individuals are limited to $5,000 statewide office candidates for primary elections and general elections, $3,000 for run-off elections, and $1,000 for nonelection years; $2,000 for other offices for primary and general elections and $1,000 for run-off elections and in non-election years. Contributions by regulated industries to those who regulate them are generally prohibited. Anonymous contributions are prohibited.
Fundraising Limits: Candidates are not limited to the amount they are allowed to raise.
Online Filing: Yes
Reporting Cycle Dates: Reports must be filed twice before and once after the primary election and once before the general election as well as year-end reports.

LOBBYING GUIDELINES

All lobbyists are required to register. They then must submit reports for each of the following time periods by the date indicated:

January 1–January 31	file by February 5
February 1–February 28	file by March 5
March 1–March 31	file by April 5
April 1–April 30	file by May 5
May 1–July 31	file by August 5
August 1–December 31	file by January 5

BALLOT INITIATIVES AND REFERENDUM

Referendum: No
Ballot Initiative: No
Recall Election: Yes

Hawaii

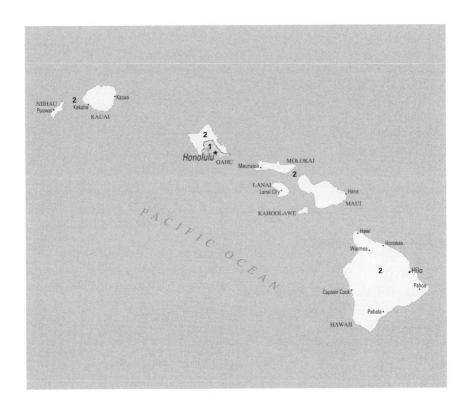

STATE VOTER TURNOUT

Population: 1,285,498
Registered Voters
   2000: 637,349
   2002: 551,156
   2004: 647,238
   2006: 662,728
   2008: 691,356
Turnout
   2000: 39.9% (Highest Office/Voting-Age Pop.): 367,951 / 921,229
   2002: 40.2% (Highest Office/Voting-Age Pop.): 382,110 / 946,680
   2004: 44.1% (Highest Office/Voting-Age Pop.): 429,013 / 972,477
   2006: 34.6% (Highest Office/Voting-Age Pop.): 344,315 / 955,937
   2008: 66.0% (Highest Office/Voting-Age Pop.): 456,064 / 691,356
Youth Turnout (18–29 years old)
   2000: 23%
   2002: 20%
   2004: 34%
   2006: 21%
   2008: 31%

STATEWIDE ELECTION OUTCOMES

Presidential Vote 2004: 431,662 votes cast
   Bush (R)   45.0%
   Kerry (D)   53.7%
Presidential Vote 2008: 456,064 votes cast
   Obama (D)   71.5%
   McCain (R)   26.4%
Gubernatorial Vote 2006: 348,751 votes cast
   Lingle (R)   61.7%
   Iwase (D)   34.9%
Electoral College Votes: 4

VOTING REGULATIONS

Residency Requirements: Hawaii resident for at least one day.
Absentee Ballot: Yes
   Criteria: Available to all voters. Application must be received by September 13, 2008, at 4:30 p.m. for the 2008 general election.

Advance Voting: Yes
   Criteria: Early in-person absentee voting available Monday through Saturday between 8:00 a.m. and 4:00 p.m.
Provisional Balloting: Yes
Vote by Phone: No
Registration Deadline: 30 days prior to election
Secretary of State Website: http://hawaii.gov/elections/

CANDIDATE REGULATIONS

Qualifications
   Governor: 30 years old, state resident for 5 years
   State Senator: 18 years old, district resident, state resident for 3 years
   State Representative: 18 years old, district resident, state resident for 3 years
Filing Fees
   Governor: $250
   State Senate: $250
   State House: $250
Filing Deadlines
   Presidential Primary: n/a (Caucus on February 19 for Democrats and January 25–February 7 for Republicans)
   Independent/Third Party in Presidential Election: September 5, 4:30 p.m.
   Congressional Primary: July 20, 2010
   Independent/Third Party in General Election: July 20, 2010
Online Filing: No
Petition Signature Requirements:
   Major Party: President: 691 (One-tenth of 1% of registered voters during the last general election)
   Minor Party: President: 4,561 (1% of votes cast in last presidential election)

JUDICIAL ELECTIONS

Justice Chosen: At large
Method of Selection
   Unexpired Term: Gubernatorial appointment from judicial nominating commission with consent of the legislature.
   Full Term: Gubernatorial appointment from judicial nominating commission with consent of the legislature.
No. of Judges: 5

Terms: 10 years
Method of Retention: Judicial nominating commission appoints

PRIMARY ELECTION PROCESS

Presidential
  Type: Caucus/Closed
  Date: Democrats: February 19, 2208; Republicans: May 17, 2008
State
  Type: Caucus/Closed
  Date: September 18, 2010

STATE CAMPAIGN FINANCE

Contribution Regulations: Individuals and non-party entities are limited to $2,000 for 2-year offices; $4,000 for 4-year offices; $6,000 for statewide offices in any election period; $1,000 to independent expenditure committees; $25,000 to political parties for a 2-year election period; and $50,000 to a national party. Candidates and their family members are limited to a total of $50,000 in any election year. Anonymous contributions are prohibited.
Fundraising Limits: There is a voluntary expenditure limitation that must be submitted to the Campaign Spending Commission; limitations correlate to the office and amount of registered voters.
Online Filing: Yes
Reporting Cycle Dates: Reports must be filed before and after each election with supplemental reports in the event of a surplus or deficit more than $250.

LOBBYING GUIDELINES

All lobbyists must register with the State Ethics Commission within 5 days of becoming a lobbyist and file reports on March 31, May 31, and January 31 each year.

BALLOT INITIATIVES AND REFERENDUM

Referendum: No
Ballot Initiative: No
Recall Election: No

Idaho

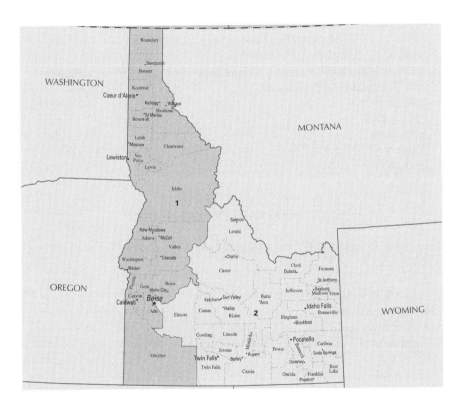

STATE VOTER TURNOUT

Population: 1,429,096
Registered Voters
    2000: 728,085
    2002: 679,535
    2004: 915,637
    2006: 764,880
    2008: 861,869
Turnout
    2000: 53.5% (Highest Office/Voting-Age Pop.): 501,615 / 935,883
    2002: 42.0% (Highest Office/Voting-Age Pop.): 411,477 / 974,057
    2004: 58.7% (Highest Office/Voting-Age Pop.): 598,376 / 1,018,931
    2006: 42.0% (Highest Office/Voting-Age Pop.): 450,832 / 1,073,799
    2008: 61.1% (Highest Office/Voting-Age Pop.): 667,506 / 1,092,000
Youth Turnout (18–29 years old)
    2000: 40%
    2002: 24%
    2004: 49%
    2006: 30%
    2008: 46%

STATEWIDE ELECTION OUTCOMES

Presidential Vote 2004: 1,883,449 votes cast
    Bush (R)   62.5%
    Kerry (D)   36.8%
Presidential Vote 2008: 655,032 votes cast
    Obama (D)   36.1%
    McCain (R)   61.5%
Gubernatorial Vote 2006: 450,832 votes cast
    Otter (R)   52.7%
    Brady (D)   44.1%
Electoral College Votes: 4

VOTING REGULATIONS

Residency Requirements: Resident of Idaho and county for 30 days prior to election.
Absentee Ballot: Yes

Criteria: Available for all voters. May be requested up to 6 days before election.
Advance Voting: Yes
   Criteria: Early in-person absentee voting available; times vary by county.
Provisional Balloting: Yes
Vote by Phone: No
Registration Deadline: 25 days prior to election
Secretary of State Website: http://www.idsos.state.id.us/elect/eleindex.htm

CANDIDATE REGULATIONS

Qualifications
   Governor: 30 years, state resident for 2 years
   State Senator: 18 years old, district and state resident for 1 year
   State Representative: 18 years old, district and state resident for 1 year
Filing Fees
   Governor: $300
   State Senate: $30
   State House: $30
Filing Deadlines
   Presidential Primary: March 21
   Independent/Third Party in Presidential Election: August 24
   Congressional Primary: March 19, 2010
   Independent/Third Party in General Election: March 19, 2010
Online Filing: No
Petition Signature Requirements
   Major Party: President: 11,968 signatures
   Minor Party: President: 5,984 signatures

JUDICIAL ELECTIONS

Justice Chosen: At large
Method of Selection
   Unexpired Term: Gubernatorial appointment from judicial nominating commission.
   Full Term: Nonpartisan election
No. of Judges: 5
Terms: 6 years
Method of Retention: Nonpartisan election

PRIMARY ELECTION PROCESS

Presidential
   Type: Democrats: Caucus/Open; Republicans: Primary/Open
   Date: Democrats: February 5, 2008; Republicans: May 27, 2008
State
   Type: Democrats: Caucus/Open; Republicans: Primary/Open
   Date: May 25, 2010

STATE CAMPAIGN FINANCE

Contribution Regulations: Individuals, corporations, political action committees, and other legal entities are limited to $5,000 for statewide elections, and $1,000 for legislative, judicial or auditorium district, county and city office. State political parties are limited to $10,000 for statewide elections and $2,000 for all other candidate elections.
Fundraising Limits: Candidates are not limited to the amount they are allowed to raise.
Online Filing: No
Reporting Cycle Dates: Reports must be filed before and after each election for those involved and on October 10 for unexpended balances.

LOBBYING GUIDELINES

All lobbyists must register and file annual, semiannual, and monthly reports with the Secretary of State.

BALLOT INITIATIVES AND REFERENDUM

Referendum: Yes
Ballot Initiative: Yes
Recall Election: Yes

ILLINOIS

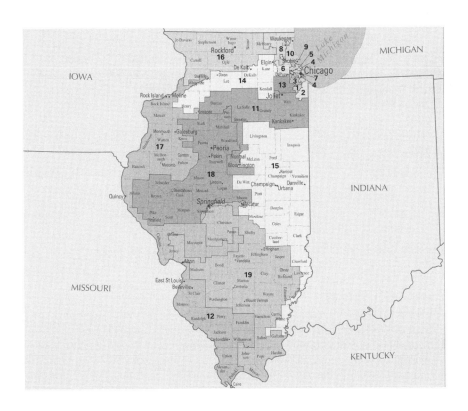

STATE VOTER TURNOUT

Population: 12,852,548
Registered Voters
  2000: 7,129,026
  2002: 7,003,115
  2004: 7,195,882
  2006: 7,375,688
  2008: 7,789,500
Turnout
  2000: 51.4% (Highest Office/Voting-Age Pop.): 1,672,551 / 3,334,714
  2002: 37.7% (Highest Office/Voting-Age Pop.): 3,538,883 / 9,354,344
  2004: 55.7% (Highest Office/Voting-Age Pop.): 5,274,322 / 9,472,200
  2006: 36.3% (Highest Office/Voting-Age Pop.): 3,486,671 / 9,600,372
  2008: 56.7% (Highest Office/Voting-Age Pop.): 5,577,509 / 9,745,274
Youth Turnout (18–29 years old)
  2000: 45%
  2002: 23%
  2004: 50%
  2006: 23%
  2008: 51%

STATEWIDE ELECTION OUTCOMES

Presidential Vote 2004: 5,274,295 votes cast
  Bush (R)   44.5%
  Kerry (D)   54.8%
Presidential Vote 2008: 5,522,371 votes cast
  Obama (D)   61.9%
  McCain (R)   36.8%
Gubernatorial Vote 2006: 3,487,989 votes cast
  Blagojevich (D)   49.8%
  Topinka (R)   39.3%
Electoral College Votes: 21

VOTING REGULATIONS

Residency Requirements: Precinct resident for 30 days
Absentee Ballot: Yes
  Criteria: Available for voters unable to be present at polls on day of
  election.

Advance Voting: Yes
    Criteria: Available from the 22nd through the 5th day prior to election.
Provisional Balloting: Yes
Vote by Phone: No
Registration Deadline: 27 days prior to election (late registration also available up to 14 days prior to election).
Secretary of State Website: http://www.elections.state.il.us/

CANDIDATE REGULATIONS

Qualifications
    Governor: 25 years old, state resident for 3 years
    State Senator: 21 years old, district resident for 2 years
    State Representative: 21 years old, district resident for 2 years
Filing Fees
    Governor: $0
    State Senate: $0
    State House: $0
Filing Deadlines
    Presidential Primary: November 5 (Democrats); December 5 (Republicans)
    Independent/Third Party in Presidential Election: June 23
    Congressional Primary: November 2, 2010
    Independent/Third Party in General Election: June 21, 2010
Online Filing: No
Petition Signature Requirements
    Major Party: President: No requirement
    Minor Party: President: 25,000 or 1% of votes cast in last statewide general election.

JUDICIAL ELECTIONS

Justice Chosen: By district
Method of Selection
    Unexpired Term: Court Selection
    Full Term: Partisan election
No. of Judges: 7
Terms: 10 years
Method of Retention: Retention election

PRIMARY ELECTION PROCESS

Presidential
  Type: Primary/Open
  Date: February 5, 2008
State
  Type: Primary/Open
  Date: February 2, 2010

STATE CAMPAIGN FINANCE

Contribution Regulations: Anonymous contributions are prohibited.
Fundraising Limits: Candidates for the Citizens Utility Board who spend more than $2,500 are not eligible for a state-sponsored candidate informational mailing.
Online Filing: No
Reporting Cycle Dates: Reports must be filed with the State Board of Elections the 15th day before each election and complete before the 30th day before each primary or general election. Additional reports must be filed by July 31 and January 31.

LOBBYING GUIDELINES

All lobbyists are required to register with the Secretary of State within two business days of being employed and file reports on or before January 31 and July 31.

BALLOT INITIATIVES AND REFERENDUM

Referendum: No
Ballot Initiative: Yes
Recall Election: No

INDIANA

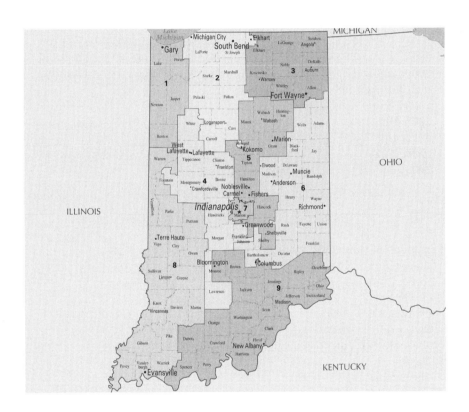

STATE VOTER TURNOUT

Population: 6,345,289
Registered Voters
   2000: 4,000,809
   2002: 4,008,636
   2004: 4,296,602
   2006: 4,295,687
   2008: 4,514,759
Turnout
   2000: 48.3% (Highest Office/Voting-Age Pop.): 2,182,295 / 4,527,527
   2002: 33.3% (Highest Office/Voting-Age Pop.): 1,521,353 / 4,586,996
   2004: 53.0% (Highest Office/Voting-Age Pop.): 2,468,002 / 4,655,046
   2006: 35.2% (Highest Office/Voting-Age Pop.): 1,666,922 / 4,732,010
   2008: 57.3% (Highest Office/Voting-Age Pop.): 2,805,986 / 4,803,224
Youth Turnout (18–29 years old)
   2000: 35%
   2002: 19%
   2004: 41%
   2006: 23%
   2008: 48%

STATEWIDE ELECTION OUTCOMES

Presidential Vote 2004: 2,468,002 votes cast
   Bush (R)   59.9%
   Kerry (D)   39.3%
Presidential Vote 2008: 2,751,054 votes cast
   Obama (D)   49.9%
   McCain (R)   48.9%
Gubernatorial Vote 2008: 2,703,752 votes cast
   Daniels (R)   57.8%
   Thompson (D)   40.0%
Electoral College Votes: 11

VOTING REGULATIONS

Residency Requirements: Precinct resident for 30 days
Absentee Ballot: Yes
   Criteria: Available for voters who are unavoidably absent from polls
   for all 12 hours they are open; election officials; 65 years of age or older;

participating in the address confidentiality program; or for those who have disabilities.

Advance Voting: Yes

Criteria: Starts 29 days prior to election and ends at 12 p.m. on the day before election.

Provisional Balloting: Yes

Vote by Phone: No

Registration Deadline: 28 days prior to election

Secretary of State Website: http://www.in.gov/sos/elections/

CANDIDATE REGULATIONS

Qualifications

Governor: 30 years old, state resident for 5 years, U.S. citizen for 5 years

State Senator: 25 years old, district resident for 1 year, state resident for 2 years

State Representative: 21 years old, district resident for 1 year, state resident for 2 years

Filing Fees

Governor: $0

State Senate: $0

State House: $0

Filing Deadlines

Presidential Primary: February 22, 12:00 p.m.

Independent/Third Party in Presidential Election: June 30, 12:00 p.m.

Congressional Primary: February 16, 2010, 12:00 p.m.

Independent/Third Party in General Election: June 30, 2010, 12:00 p.m.

Online Filing: No

Petition Signature Requirements

Major Party: President: No requirement

Minor Party: President: 32,742 (2% of votes cast for Secretary of State in last election)

JUDICIAL ELECTIONS

Justice Chosen: At large

Method of Selection

Unexpired Term: Gubernatorial appointment from judicial nominating commission.

Full Term: Gubernatorial appointment from judicial nominating.

No. of Judges: 5

Terms: 10 years (Initial term is 2 years, retention is 10)
Method of Retention: Retention election

PRIMARY ELECTION PROCESS

Presidential
  Type: Primary/Open
  Date: May 6, 2008
State
  Type: Primary/Open
  Date: May 4, 2010

STATE CAMPAIGN FINANCE

Contribution Regulations: Individuals and organizations other than corporations and labor unions may contribute unlimited amounts. Corporations and labor unions are limited to $5,000 for statewide candidates or state party central committees and $2,000 for House legislative caucuses, Senate legislative caucuses, all House candidates, all Senate candidates, school board and local office candidates, or non-state party candidates (totaling $22,000 a year).
Fundraising Limits: Candidates are not limited to the amount of funds they can raise.
Online Filing: Yes
Reporting Cycle Dates: Reports must be filed by the 3rd Wednesday in January annually as well as 25 days before the primary election and 25 days before a general election.

LOBBYING GUIDELINES

All lobbyists are required to register within 15 days of being employed to be renewed annually. Reports must be filed by May 31 and November 30.

BALLOT INITIATIVES AND REFERENDUM

Referendum: No
Ballot Initiative: No
Recall Election: No

IOWA

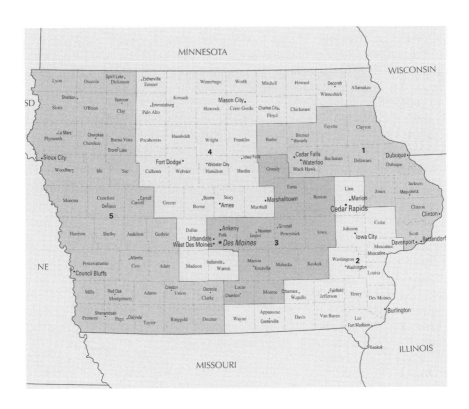

STATE VOTER TURNOUT

Population: 2,988,046
Registered Voters
  2000: 1,841,346
  2002: 1,121,908
  2004: 2,226,721
  2006: 2,077,239
  2008: 2,111,809
Turnout
  2000: 59.6% (Highest Office/Voting-Age Pop.): 1,315,563 / 2,198,024
  2002: 45.7% (Highest Office/Voting-Age Pop.): 1,023,075 / 2,213,808
  2004: 67.4% (Highest Office/Voting-Age Pop.): 1,506,908 / 2,237,158
  2006: 46.3% (Highest Office/Voting-Age Pop.): 1,048,033 / 2,265,860
  2008: 67.3% (Highest Office/Voting-Age Pop.): 1,543,662 / 2,294,375
Youth Turnout (18–29 years old)
  2000: 50%
  2002: 23%
  2004: 60%
  2006: 27%
  2008: 63%

STATEWIDE ELECTION OUTCOMES

Presidential Vote 2004: 1,059,064 votes cast
  Bush (R)   59.9%
  Kerry (D)   39.3%
Presidential Vote 2008: 1,537,123 votes cast
  Obama (D)   53.9%
  McCain (R)   44.4%
Gubernatorial Vote 2008: 1,059,064 votes cast
  Culver (D)   53.7%
  Nussle (R)   44.1%
Electoral College Votes: 7

VOTING REGULATIONS

Residency Requirements: Iowa resident
Absentee Ballot: Yes
  Criteria: Available for all voters. Ballots must be requested by 5:00 p.m.
  on Friday prior to election.

Advance Voting: Yes
    Criteria: Available beginning 40 days prior to election and ending the Monday prior to election.
Provisional Balloting: Yes
Vote by Phone: No
Registration Deadline: 10 days prior to primary or general election, 11 days prior to other elections, both by 5:00 p.m. Registrations by mail must be postmarked 15 days prior to election.
Secretary of State Website: http://www.sos.state.ia.us/elections/index.html

CANDIDATE REGULATIONS

Qualifications
    Governor: 30 years old, state resident for 2 years
    State Senator: 25 years old, district resident for 60 days, state resident for 1 year
    State Representative: 21 years old, district resident for 60 days, state resident for 1 year
Filing Fees
    Governor: $0
    State Senate: $0
    State House: $0
Filing Deadlines
    Presidential Primary: n/a (Caucus on January 3)
    Independent/Third Party in Presidential Election: August 15
    Congressional Primary: March 19, 2010 (5:00 p.m.)
    Independent/Third Party in General Election: August 13, 2010
Online Filing: Yes
Petition Signature Requirements
    Major Party: President: No requirement
    Minor Party: President: 1,500

JUDICIAL ELECTIONS

Justice Chosen: At large
Method of Selection
    Unexpired Term: Gubernatorial appointment from judicial nominating commission.
    Full Term: Gubernatorial appointment from judicial nominating commission.

No. of Judges: 7
Terms: 8 years
Method of Retention: Retention election

PRIMARY ELECTION PROCESS

Presidential
  Type: Democrats: Caucus/Open
            Republicans: Caucus/Semiopen
  Date: January 3, 2008
State
  Type: Democrats: Caucus/Open
            Republicans: Caucus/Semiopen
  Date: June 8, 2010

STATE CAMPAIGN FINANCE

Contribution Regulations: Insurance companies, savings and loan associations, banks, credit unions, or corporations may not contribute.
Fundraising Limits: Candidates are not limited to the amount they can raise.
Online Filing: Yes
Reporting Cycle Dates: Reports must be filed by May 19, July 19, October 19, and January 19 annually.

LOBBYING GUIDELINES

All lobbyists are required to register with the Iowa Ethics and Campaign Disclosure Board and file reports by July 31, October 31, and January 31.

BALLOT INITIATIVES AND REFERENDUM

Referendum: No
Ballot Initiative: No
Recall Election: No

Kansas

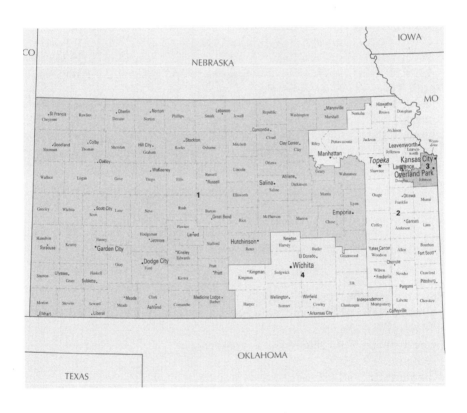

STATE VOTER TURNOUT

Population: 2,775,997
Registered Voters
  2000: 1,623,623
  2002: 1,615,698
  2004: 1,695,457
  2006: 1,663,017
  2008: 1,749,756
Turnout
  2000: 54.0% (Highest Office/Voting-Age Pop.): 1,072,216 / 1,983,910
  2002: 41.4% (Highest Office/Voting-Age Pop.): 835,692 / 2,010,382
  2004: 58.3% (Highest Office/Voting-Age Pop.): 1,187,756 / 2,036,741
  2006: 41.1% (Highest Office/Voting-Age Pop.): 849,700 / 2,068,253
  2008: 58.6% (Highest Office/Voting-Age Pop.): 1,235,872 / 2,108,894
Youth Turnout (18–29 years old)
  2000: 38%
  2002: 23%
  2004: 45%
  2006: 20%
  2008: 45%

STATEWIDE ELECTION OUTCOMES

Presidential Vote 2004: 1,187,756 votes cast
  Bush (R)   62.0%
  Kerry (D)   36.6%
Presidential Vote 2008: 1,235,872 votes cast
  Obama (D)   41.6%
  McCain (R) 56.6%
Gubernatorial Vote 2008: 849,700 votes cast
  Sebelius (D) 57.9%
  Barnett (R)   40.4%
Electoral College Votes: 6

VOTING REGULATIONS

Residency Requirements: Kansas resident
Absentee Ballot: Yes
  Criteria: Available through advance voting process.
Advance Voting: Yes

Criteria: Begins 20 days prior to election. Ballots must be received by close of polls on day of election.
Provisional Balloting: Yes
Vote by Phone: No
Registration Deadline: 15 days prior to election
Secretary of State Website: http://www.kssos.org/elections/elections.html

CANDIDATE REGULATIONS

Qualifications
  Governor: None
  State Senator: 18 years old, district resident
  State Representative: 18 years old, district resident
Filing Fees
  Governor: Information unavailable (usually 1% of annual salary).
  State Senate: $130
  State House: $105
Filing Deadlines
  Presidential Primary: n/a (Democratic Caucus on February 5, Republican Caucus on February 9).
  Independent/Third Party in Presidential Election: August 4, 12:00 p.m.
  Congressional Primary: June 10, 2010, 12:00 p.m.
  Independent/Third Party in General Election: June 10, 2010, 12:00 p.m. (Third Party), August 2, 2010, 12:00 p.m. (Independent)
Online Filing: No
Petition Signature Requirements
  Major Party: President: 16,994 (2% of votes cast in last gubernatorial election)
  Minor Party: President: 5,000

JUDICIAL ELECTIONS

Justice Chosen: At large
Method of Selection
  Unexpired Term: Gubernatorial appointment from judicial nominating commission.
  Full Term: Gubernatorial appointment from judicial nominating commission.
No. of Judges: 7

Terms: 6 years
Method of Retention: Retention election

PRIMARY ELECTION PROCESS

Presidential
  Type: Caucus/Closed
  Date: Democrats: February 5, 2008; Republicans: February 9, 2008
State
  Type: Caucus/Closed
  Date: August 3, 2010

STATE CAMPAIGN FINANCE

Contribution Regulations: Individuals are limited to contributions of $2,000 for statewide candidates, $1,000 for state senate candidates, and $500 for candidates for other offices. Political parties may contribute an unlimited amount in an uncontested primary or general election. Anonymous contributions more than $10 are prohibited. Cash contributions are limited to $100.
Fundraising Limits: Candidates are not limited to the amount of funds they can raise.
Online Filing: No
Reporting Cycle Dates: Reports must be filed with the Secretary of State before the 8th day preceding the primary election, the 11th day preceding the general election, January 10, and annually by February 15.

LOBBYING GUIDELINES

All lobbyists are required to register with the Secretary of State annually by October 1 and file reports by the 10th day of February, March, April, May, September, and January.

BALLOT INITIATIVES AND REFERENDUM

Referendum: No
Ballot Initiative: No
Recall Election: Yes

KENTUCKY

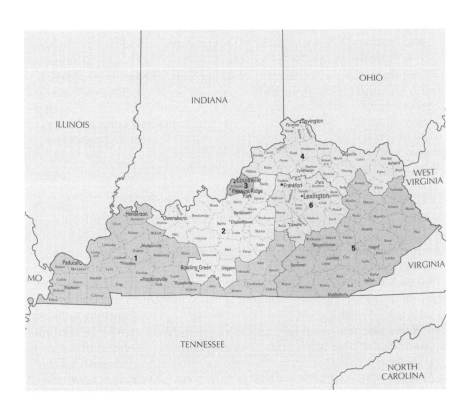

STATE VOTER TURNOUT

Population: 4,241,474
Registered Voters
  2000: 2,556,815
  2002: 2,649,084
  2004: 2,794,286
  2006: 2,766,288
  2008: 2,906,809
Turnout
  2000: 50.4% (Highest Office/Voting-Age Pop.): 1,544,107 / 3,060,881
  2002: 36.4% (Highest Office/Voting-Age Pop.): 1,131,313 / 3,102,696
  2004: 56.9% (Highest Office/Voting-Age Pop.): 1,795,860 / 3,154,762
  2006: 39.0% (Highest Office/Voting-Age Pop.): 1,253,526 / 3,213,141
  2008: 50.3% (Highest Office/Voting-Age Pop.): 1,826,508 / 3,269,074
Youth Turnout (18–29 years old)
  2000: 43%
  2002: 30%
  2004: 60%
  2006: 28%
  2008: 50%

STATEWIDE ELECTION OUTCOMES

Presidential Vote 2004: 1,795,860 votes cast
  Bush (R)   59.6%
  Kerry (D)   39.7%
Presidential Vote 2008: 1,826,508 votes cast
  Obama (D)   41.2%
  McCain (R) 57.4%
Gubernatorial Vote 2007: 1,055,325 votes cast
  Beshear (D) 58.7%
  Fletcher (R) 41.3%
Electoral College Votes: 8

VOTING REGULATIONS

Residency Requirements: Kentucky resident for 28 days.
Absentee Ballot: Yes

Criteria: Available for voters who are of advanced age; have a disability or illness; are absent from their county or state due to studies, vacation, or work; or are incarcerated but not yet convicted.

Advance Voting: Yes

Criteria: Available for eligible voters 12 (or possibly more) working days prior to election.

Provisional Balloting: Yes

Vote by Phone: No

Registration Deadline: 28 days prior to election

Secretary of State Website: http://www.sos.ky.gov/elections/

CANDIDATE REGULATIONS

Qualifications

Governor: 30 years old, state resident for 6 years

State Senator: 30 years old, district resident for 1 year, state resident for 6 years

State Representative: 24 years old, county/town/city resident for 1 year, state resident for 2 years

Filing Fees

Governor: $500

State Senate: $200

State House: $200

Filing Deadlines

Presidential Primary: January 29, 4:00 p.m.

Independent/Third Party in Presidential Election: September 5, 4:00 p.m.

Congressional Primary: January 26, 2010, at 4:00 p.m.

Independent/Third Party in General Election: August 10, 2010, 4:00 p.m.

Online Filing: No

Petition Signature Requirements

Major Party: President: No requirement

Minor Party: President: 5,000

JUDICIAL ELECTIONS

Justice Chosen: By district

Method of Selection

Unexpired Term: Gubernatorial appointment from judicial nominating commission.

Full Term: Nonpartisan election
No. of Judges: 7
Terms: 8 years
Method of Retention: Nonpartisan election

PRIMARY ELECTION PROCESS

Presidential:
   Type: Primary/Closed
   Date: May 20, 2008
State
   Type: Primary/Open
   Date: May 8, 2010

STATE CAMPAIGN FINANCE

Contribution Regulations: Individuals are limited to contributions of $2,000 for statewide candidates, $1,000 for state senate candidates, and $500 for candidates for other offices. Political parties may contribute an unlimited amount in an uncontested primary or general election. Anonymous contributions over $10 are prohibited. Cash contributions are limited to $100.
Fundraising Limits: Candidates are not limited to the amount they are allowed to raise.
Online Filing: No
Reporting Cycle Dates: Reports must be filed with the Secretary of State before the 8th day preceding the primary election, the 11th day preceding the general election, January 10, and annually by February 15.

LOBBYING GUIDELINES

All lobbyists are required to register with the Secretary of State annually by October 1 and file reports by the 10th day of February, March, April, May, September, and January.

BALLOT INITIATIVES AND REFERENDUM

Referendum: Yes
Ballot Initiative: No
Recall Election: No

LOUISIANA

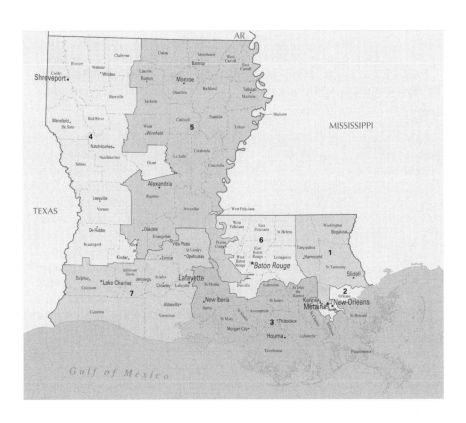

STATE VOTER TURNOUT

Population: 4,293,204
Registered Voters
  2000: 2,730,380
  2002: 2,524,187
  2004: 2,932,142
  2006: 2,890,891
  2008: 2,908,342
Turnout
  2000: 54.2% (Highest Office/Voting-Age Pop.): 1,765,656 / 3,254,592
  2002: 37.8% (Highest Office/Voting-Age Pop.): 1,246,333 / 3,282,887
  2004: 58.5% (Highest Office/Voting-Age Pop.): 1,943,106 / 3,321,850
  2006: 28.3% (Highest Office/Voting-Age Pop.): 902,498 / 3,188,765
  2008: 59.4% (Highest Office/Voting-Age Pop.): 1,980,377 / 3,332,549
Youth Turnout (18–29 years old)
  2000: 50%
  2002: 28%
  2004: 52%
  2006: 18%
  2008: 56%

STATEWIDE ELECTION OUTCOMES

Presidential Vote 2004: 1,943,106 votes cast
  Bush (R)   56.7%
  Kerry (D)   42.2%
Presidential Vote 2008: 1,960,761 votes cast
  Obama (D)   39.9%
  McCain (R)   58.6%
Gubernatorial Vote 2007: 1,297,840 votes cast
  Jindal (R)   53.9%
  Boasso (D)   17.5%
Electoral College Votes: 9

VOTING REGULATIONS

Residency Requirements: Louisiana resident
Absentee Ballot: Yes
  Criteria: Available for voters specifying why they expect to be absent
  from the polls on day of election. May be requested beginning 60 days
  prior to election.

Advance Voting: Yes
  Criteria: Specific dates and times set by parish registrar.
Provisional Balloting: Yes
Vote by Phone: No
Registration Deadline: 30 days prior to election
Secretary of State Website: http://www.sos.louisiana.gov/

CANDIDATE REGULATIONS

Qualifications
  Governor: 25 years old, state resident for 5 years, U.S. citizen for 5 years
  State Senator: 18 years old, district resident for 1 year, state resident for 2 years
  State Representative: 18 years old, district resident for 1 year, state resident for 2 years
Filing Fees
  Governor: $750 (Additional fee for Republican and Democratic candidates is $375)
  State Senate: $300 (Additional fee for Republican and Democratic candidates is $150)
  State House: $225 (Additional fee for Republican and Democratic candidates is $112.50)
Filing Deadlines
  Presidential Primary: December 14
  Independent/Third Party in Presidential Election: September 2
  Congressional Primary: July 9, 2010
  Independent/Third Party in General Election: July 9, 2010
Online Filing: No
Petition Signature Requirements
  Major Party: President: 1,000 (Registered Voters)
  Minor Party: President: Pay $500 fee

JUDICIAL ELECTIONS

Justice Chosen: By district
Method of Selection
  Unexpired Term: Court selection (no expired terms).
  Full Term: Partisan election (blanket primary—top two vote-getters compete in general election).
No. of Judges: 7

Terms: 10 years
Method of Retention: Partisan election (blanket primary—top two vote-getters compete in general election).

PRIMARY ELECTION PROCESS

Presidential
   Type: Primary/Closed
   Date: May 9, 2008
State
   Type: Primary/Closed
   Date: August 28, 2010

STATE CAMPAIGN FINANCE

Contribution Regulations: Cash and anonymous contributions are prohibited. Limits on contributions are as follows: $5,000 to a candidate for major office including statewide offices; $2,500 to a candidate for district office including members of the state legislature; $1,000 to a candidate for any other office. Political committees with more than 250 members contributing at least $50 each during the preceding calendar year are limited to $10,000 to a major office candidate, $5,000 to a district office candidate, and $2,000 to a candidate for any other office.
Fundraising Limits: Candidates are limited to the amount they may accept from all political committees combined for the primary and general elections as follows: $80,000 for a major office candidate; $60,000 for a district office candidate; and $20,000 for a candidate for any other office.
Online Filing: Yes, required for statewide candidates with more than $50,000 in receipts or loans.
Reporting Cycle Dates: Reports must be filed with the Supervisory Committee on Campaign Finance Disclosure 180, 90, 30, and 10 days before the primary election, 10 days before the general election, and 40 days after the general election.

LOBBYING GUIDELINES

All lobbyists are required to register within 5 days of being employed and file reports by August 15 and February 15.

BALLOT INITIATIVES AND REFERENDUM

Referendum: No
Ballot Initiative: No
Recall Election: Yes

Maine

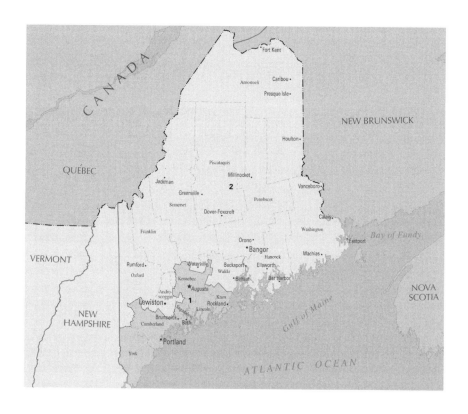

STATE VOTER TURNOUT

Population: 1,317,207
Registered Voters
  2000: 882,337
  2002: 950,059
  2004: 1,026,219
  2006: 993,748
  2008: 942,825
Turnout
  2000: 66.4% (Highest Office/Voting-Age Pop.): 651,817 / 979,356
  2002: 50.1% (Highest Office/Voting-Age Pop.): 505,190 / 1,001,556
  2004: 72.6% (Highest Office/Voting-Age Pop.): 740,752 / 1,020,050
  2006: 53.3% (Highest Office/Voting-Age Pop.): 550,865 / 1,033,632
  2008: 70.1% (Highest Office/Voting-Age Pop.): 731,163 / 1,042,872
Youth Turnout (18–29 years old)
  2000: 52%
  2002: 31%
  2004: 59%
  2006: 32%
  2008: 57%

STATEWIDE ELECTION OUTCOMES

Presidential Vote 2004: 740,752 votes cast
  Bush (R)   44.6%
  Kerry (D)   53.6%
Presidential Vote 2008: 731,163 votes cast
  Obama (D)   49.9%
  McCain (R)   48.9%
Gubernatorial Vote 2008: 550,865 votes cast
  Baldacci (D)   38.1%
  Woodcock (R)   30.2%
Electoral College Votes: 4

VOTING REGULATIONS

Residency Requirements: Resident of municipality
Absentee Ballot: Yes

Criteria: Available for all voters. May be requested beginning 3 months prior to election. Ballot must be received before close of polls on day of election.

Advance Voting: Yes

Criteria: Available as absentee in-person voting as soon as absentee ballots are available, usually 30 to 45 days prior to election.

Provisional Balloting: Yes

Vote by Phone: Yes

Registration Deadline: 21 days prior to election by mail. In-person registration available up until, and on, the day of election.

Secretary of State Website: http://www.maine.gov/sos/cec/elec/index .html

CANDIDATE REGULATIONS

Qualifications

Governor: 30 years old, state resident for 5 years, U.S. citizen for 15 years

State Senator: 25 years old, district resident for 3 months, state resident for 1 year, U.S. citizen for 5 years

State Representative: 21 years old, district resident for 3 months, state resident for 1 year, U.S. citizen for 5 years

Filing Fees

Governor: $0

State Senate: $0

State House: $0

Filing Deadlines

Presidential Primary: Democratic Caucus on February 10, Republican Caucus on February 1

Independent/Third Party in Presidential Election: August 15, 5:00 p.m.

Congressional Primary: March 15, 2010, 5:00 p.m.

Independent/Third Party in General Election: May 25, 2010, 5:00 p.m.

Online Filing: No

Petition Signature Requirements

Major Party: President: 27,544

Minor Party: President: 4,000

JUDICIAL ELECTIONS

Justice Chosen: At large
Method of Selection
Unexpired Term: Gubernatorial appointment with consent of the legislature.
Full Term: Gubernatorial appointment with consent of the legislature.
No. of Judges: 7
Terms: 7 years
Method of Retention: Unexpired Term: Gubernatorial appointment with consent of the legislature.

PRIMARY ELECTION PROCESS

Presidential
Type: Caucus/Closed
Date: Democrats: February 10, 2008; Republicans: February 1, 2008
State
Type: Caucus/Closed
Date: June 8, 2010

STATE CAMPAIGN FINANCE

Contribution Regulations: Individual contributions are limited to $25,000 total per calendar year and $1,000 per candidate per election. Contributions by political committees, corporations, and associates are limited to $5,000 per candidate per election. All contributions are limited to $500 per gubernatorial candidate and $250 for any other candidates per election. Anonymous contributions more than $10 are prohibited.
Fundraising Limits: Candidates may accept voluntary limitations of $25,000 for a State Senate race and $5,000 for a State House of Representatives' race.
Online Filing: No
Reporting Cycle Dates: Reports must be filed on January 15, April 10, July 15, and October 10. General and primary election reports must be filed on the 6th day before the date on which the election is held and on the 42nd day after the election.

LOBBYING GUIDELINES

All lobbyists are required to register within 15 business days of being employed and pay a registration fee of $200 for each lobbyist and $100 for each lobbyist associate. During the period the Legislature is in session, monthly reports must be filed by the 15th of each month. Annual reports are due 30 days after the end of the year.

BALLOT INITIATIVES AND REFERENDUM

Referendum: Yes
Ballot Initiative: Yes
Recall Election: No

MARYLAND

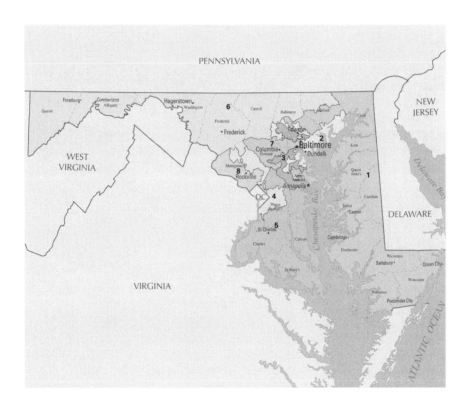

STATE VOTER TURNOUT

Population: 5,618,344
Registered Voters
2000: 2,715,366
2002: 2,768,946
2004: 3,105,370
2006: 3,142,591
2008: 3,428,935
Turnout
2000: 51.0% (Highest Office/Voting-Age Pop.): 2,025,480 / 3,972,806
2002: 41.6% (Highest Office/Voting-Age Pop.): 1,704,560 / 4,081,754
2004: 57.2% (Highest Office/Voting-Age Pop.): 2,386,705 / 7,172,530
2006: 42.2% (Highest Office/Voting-Age Pop.): 1,788,316 / 4,242,214
2008: 60.9% (Highest Office/Voting-Age Pop.): 2,622,391 / 4,304,170
Youth Turnout (18–29 years old)
2000: 40%
2002: 24%
2004: 50%
2006: 33%
2008: 56%

STATEWIDE ELECTION OUTCOMES

Presidential Vote 2004: 2,384,238 votes cast
Bush (R)   43.0%
Kerry (D)   56.0%
Presidential Vote 2008: 2,622,391 votes cast
Obama (D)   61.9%
McCain (R)   36.5%
Gubernatorial Vote 2006: 1,787,049 votes cast
O'Malley (D) 52.7%
Ehrlich (R)   46.2%
Electoral College Votes: 10

VOTING REGULATIONS

Residency Requirements: Maryland resident
Absentee Ballot: Yes

Criteria: Available for all voters. Must be requested usually 7 days prior to election, by 4:30 p.m. if by mail or by 11:59 p.m. if by fax. Ballots must be returned before 8:00 p.m. on day of election.
Advance Voting: No
Provisional Balloting: Yes
Vote by Phone: No
Registration Deadline: 21 days prior to election, by 9:00 p.m.
Secretary of State Website: http://www.elections.state.md.us/

CANDIDATE REGULATIONS

Qualifications
    Governor: 30 years old, state resident for 5 years
    State Senator: 25 years old, district resident for 6 months, state resident for 1 year
    State Representative: 21 years old, district resident for 6 months, state resident for 1 year
Filing Fees
    Governor: $290
    State Senate: $50
    State House: $50
Filing Deadlines
    Presidential Primary: December 3
    Independent/Third Party in Presidential Election: August 4
    Congressional Primary: July 6, 2010
    Independent/Third Party in General Election: August 2, 2010
Online Filing: No
Petition Signature Requirements
    Major Party: President: 10,000
    Minor Party: President: 31,102

JUDICIAL ELECTIONS

Justice Chosen: By district
Method of Selection
    Unexpired Term: Gubernatorial appointment from judicial nominating commission with consent of the legislature.
    Full Term: Gubernatorial appointment from judicial nominating commission with consent of the legislature.
No. of Judges: 7
Terms: 10 years

Method of Retention: Retention election

PRIMARY ELECTION PROCESS

Presidential
  Type: Primary/Closed
  Date: February 12, 2008
State
  Type: Primary/Closed
  Date: September 14, 2010

STATE CAMPAIGN FINANCE

Contribution Regulations: Individuals are limited to a contribution of $4,000 per candidate per election and $10,000 total in contributions in a 4-year election cycle. Political committees are limited to $6,000 per candidate in the 4-year election cycle. Political party contributions are not limited. Cash contributions are limited to $100 and anonymous contributions are prohibited.
Fundraising Limits: Candidates are not limited in the amount they can raise.
Online Filing: Yes
Reporting Cycle Dates: Reports must be filed by the 4th Tuesday before the primary election, the 2nd Friday before the election, the 3rd Tuesday after the general election, 6 months after the last general election, 1 year after the general election, and annually on the anniversary of the general election.

LOBBYING GUIDELINES

All lobbyists are required to register within 5 days of being employed and file reports by May 31 and November 30.

BALLOT INITIATIVES AND REFERENDUM

Referendum: Yes
Ballot Initiative: No
Recall Election: No

Massachusetts

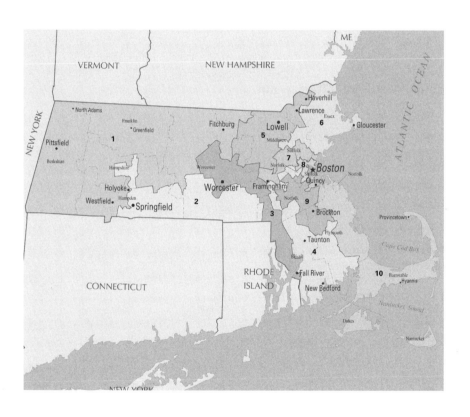

STATE VOTER TURNOUT

Population: 6,449,755
Registered Voters
  2000: 2,715,366
  2002: 2,768,946
  2004: 3,105,370
  2006: 3,142,591
  2008: 4,220,488
Turnout
  2000: 51.0% (Highest Office/Voting-Age Pop.): 2,025,480 / 3,972,806
  2002: 41.6% (Highest Office/Voting-Age Pop.): 1,704,560 / 4,081,754
  2004: 57.2% (Highest Office/Voting-Age Pop.): 2,386,705 / 7,172,530
  2006: 42.2% (Highest Office/Voting-Age Pop.): 1,788,316 / 4,242,214
  2008: 61.0% (Highest Office/Voting-Age Pop.): 3,102,995 / 5,088,946
Youth Turnout (18–29 years old)
  2000: 43%
  2002: 23%
  2004: 51%
  2006: 34%
  2008: 48%

STATEWIDE ELECTION OUTCOMES

Presidential Vote 2004: 2,912,388 votes cast
  Bush (R)   36.8%
  Kerry (D)   61.9%
Presidential Vote 2008: 3,102,995 votes cast
  Obama (D)   61.4%
  McCain (R)   35.7%
Gubernatorial Vote 2006: 2,243,835 votes cast
  Patrick (D)   55.0%
  Healy (R)   35.0%
Electoral College Votes: 10

VOTING REGULATIONS

Residency Requirements: Massachusetts resident
Absentee Ballot: Yes

Criteria: Available for voters absent from city or town on day of election, or those who are disabled or restricted from voting at polls due to religious beliefs. Must be requested by 12:00 p.m. on the day prior to election.

Advance Voting: Yes

Criteria: Available as in-person absentee voting for those eligible for absentee ballot.

Provisional Balloting: Yes

Vote by Phone: No

Registration Deadline: 20 days prior to election

Secretary of State Website: http://www.sec.state.ma.us/ele/

CANDIDATE REGULATIONS

Qualifications
  Governor: 18 years old, state resident for 7 years
  State Senator: 18 years old, district resident, state resident for 5 years
  State Representative: 18 years old, district resident for 1 year
Filing Fees
  Governor: Information unavailable (set by local offices)
  State Senate: Information unavailable (set by local offices)
  State House: Information unavailable (set by local offices)
Filing Deadlines
  Presidential Primary: December 6
  Independent/Third Party in Presidential Election: August 26
  Congressional Primary: June 1, 2010
  Independent/Third Party in General Election: August 31, 2010
Online Filing: No
Petition Signature Requirements
  Major Party: President: 10,000
  Minor Party: President: 31,102

JUDICIAL ELECTIONS

Justice Chosen: At large
Method of Selection
  Unexpired Term: There are no expired terms.
  Full Term: Gubernatorial appointment from judicial nominating commission with approval of elected executive council.
No. of Judges: 7
Terms: To age 70
Method of Retention: Serve with good behavior.

PRIMARY ELECTION PROCESS

Presidential
  Type: Primary/Semiclosed
  Date: February 5, 2008
State
  Type: Primary/Semiclosed
  Date: September 14, 2010

STATE CAMPAIGN FINANCE

Contribution Regulations: Individuals are limited to contributions of $500 per candidate per year, $12,500 in total. Minors are limited to $25 per year. Corporations are prohibited from contributing. Political action committees and labor unions are limited to $500 in a calendar year. Cash contributions are limited to $50. Anonymous contributions are prohibited.
Fundraising Limits: Candidates are not limited the amount to which they can raise.
Online Filing: Yes
Reporting Cycle Dates: Reports must be filed by the 8th day preceding the primary election, 8th day preceding the general election, 30 days after the election, and a final report by January 10.

LOBBYING GUIDELINES

All lobbyists are required to register within 10 days of being employed and file reports by July 15 and January 15.

BALLOT INITIATIVES AND REFERENDUM

Referendum: Yes
Ballot Initiative: Yes
Recall Election: No

Michigan

STATE VOTER TURNOUT

Population: 10,071,822
Registered Voters
  2000: 6,861,342
  2002: 6,797,293
  2004: 7,164,047
  2006: 7,180,778
  2008: 7,470,764
Turnout
  2000: 57.3% (Highest Office/Voting-Age Pop.): 4,232,501 / 7,379,013
  2002: 42.3% (Highest Office/Voting-Age Pop.): 3,177,565 / 7,483,080
  2004: 63.9% (Highest Office/Voting-Age Pop.): 4,839,252 / 7,572,730
  2006: 49.9% (Highest Office/Voting-Age Pop.): 3,801,256 / 7,620,982
  2008: 65.7% (Highest Office/Voting-Age Pop.): 5,001,766 / 7,609,310
Youth Turnout (18–29 years old)
  2000: 41%
  2002: 25%
  2004: 55%
  2006: 38%
  2008: 56%

STATEWIDE ELECTION OUTCOMES

Presidential Vote 2004: 4,839,252 votes cast
  Bush (R)   47.8%
  Kerry (D)   51.2%
Presidential Vote 2008: 5,001,766 votes cast
  Obama (D)   57.4%
  McCain (R)   41.0%
Gubernatorial Vote 2006: 3,801,256 votes cast
  Granholm (D)   56.4%
  DeVos (R)   42.3%
Electoral College Votes: 17

VOTING REGULATIONS

Residency Requirements: Resident of city or township for 30 days
Absentee Ballot: Yes
  Criteria: Available for voters: 60 years of age or older, unable to vote
  without assistance at the polls, expecting to be out of town on day of

election, incarcerated but not convicted, unable to attend due to religious reasons, or appointed to work as election inspector outside of home precinct. Must be requested by 2:00 p.m. on Saturday prior to election.

Advance Voting: No
Provisional Balloting: Yes
Vote by Phone: No
Registration Deadline: 30 days prior to election
Secretary of State Website: http://www.michigan.gov/sos

CANDIDATE REGULATIONS

Qualifications
   Governor: 30 years old, state resident for 4 years
   State Senator: 21 years old, district resident
   State Representative: 21 years old, district resident
Filing Fees
   Governor: $0
   State Senate: $100 (in lieu of petition)
   State House: $100 (in lieu of petition)
Filing Deadlines
   Presidential Primary: October 23, 4:00 p.m.
   Independent/Third Party in Presidential Election: July 17
   Congressional Primary: May 11, 2010, 4:00 p.m.
   Independent/Third Party in General Election: July 15, 2010, 4:00 p.m. (Independent)
Online Filing: No
Petition Signature Requirements
   Major Party: President: 38,024 (At least 100 registered voters in half of the congressional districts)
   Minor Party: President: 38,024 (At least 100 registered voters in half of the congressional districts)

JUDICIAL ELECTIONS

Justice Chosen: At large
Method of Selection
   Unexpired Term: Gubernatorial appointment
   Full Term: Nonpartisan election (Candidate may be nominated by a political party but is elected on a nonpartisan ballot.)
No. of Judges: 7

Terms: 8 years
Method of Retention: Nonpartisan election (Candidate may be nominated by a political party but is elected on a nonpartisan ballot.)

PRIMARY ELECTION PROCESS

Presidential
   Type: Primary/Open
   Date: January 15, 2008
State
   Type: Primary/Open
   Date: August 3, 2010

STATE CAMPAIGN FINANCE

Contribution Regulations: Direct corporate, labor, and domestic dependent sovereign contributions are prohibited. Individuals are limited to contributions of $3,400 for statewide candidate, $1,000 for State Senator candidate, and $500 for State Representative candidate per election cycle. Cash contributions are limited to $20 and anonymous contributions are prohibited.
Fundraising Limits: Candidates for Governor or Lieutenant Governor who accept public financing are limited to $2 million for one election, not including incidental expenses.
Online Filing: Yes, some online filing.
Reporting Cycle Dates: Reports must be filed by July 25 or October 25.

LOBBYING GUIDELINES

All lobbyists are required to register with the Secretary of State within 15 days of being employed and file reports by January 31 and August 31.

BALLOT INITIATIVES AND REFERENDUM

Referendum: Yes
Ballot Initiative: Yes
Recall Election: Yes

MINNESOTA

STATE VOTER TURNOUT

Population: 5,197,621
Registered Voters
  2000: 3,265,324
  2002: 2,844,428
  2004: 2,977,496
  2006: 3,118,398
  2008: 3,199,134
Turnout
  2000: 66.4% (Highest Office/Voting-Age Pop.): 2,438,657 / 3,662,115
  2002: 59.7% (Highest Office/Voting-Age Pop.): 2,254,639 / 3,751,732
  2004: 73.9% (Highest Office/Voting-Age Pop.): 2,828,387 / 3,828,708
  2006: 56.4% (Highest Office/Voting-Age Pop.): 2,202,987 / 3,908,159
  2008: 73.2% (Highest Office/Voting-Age Pop.): 2,910,369 / 3,975,219
Youth Turnout (18–29 years old)
  2000: 51%
  2002: 45%
  2004: 71%
  2006: 43%
  2008: 68%

STATEWIDE ELECTION OUTCOMES

Presidential Vote 2004: 2,823,979 votes cast
  Bush (R)   47.6%
  Kerry (D)   51.1%
Presidential Vote 2008: 2,910,369 votes cast
  Obama (D)   49.9%
  McCain (R)   43.8%
Gubernatorial Vote 2006: 2,202,937 votes cast
  Pawlenty (R) 46.7%
  Hatch (D)   45.7%
Electoral College Votes: 10

VOTING REGULATIONS

Residency Requirements: Minnesota resident for 20 days
Absentee Ballot: Yes
  Criteria: Available for voters who are away from home, ill, disabled, election judges in other precincts, or are unable to be present at polls

due to religious beliefs. Must be received by 5:00 p.m. one day prior to election.

Advance Voting: Yes

Criteria: Available as in-person absentee voting beginning 30 days prior to election.

Provisional Balloting: No (but Election Day registration is available).

Vote by Phone: No

Registration Deadline: 20 days prior to election

Secretary of State Website: http://www.sos.state.mn.us/home/index.asp?page=4

CANDIDATE REGULATIONS

Qualifications

Governor: 25 years old, state resident for 1 year

State Senator: 21 years old, district resident for 6 months, state resident for 1 year

State Representative: 21 years old, district resident for 6 months, state resident for 1 year

Filing Fees

Governor: $300

State Senate: $100

State House: $100

Filing Deadlines

Presidential Primary: n/a (Caucus on February 5)

Independent/Third Party in Presidential Election: September 9

Congressional Primary: July 20, 2010

Independent/Third Party in General Election: July 20, 2010

Online Filing: No

Petition Signature Requirements

Major Party: President: No requirement

Minor Party: President: 2,000

JUDICIAL ELECTIONS

Justice Chosen: At large

Method of Selection

Unexpired Term: Gubernatorial appointment

Full Term: Nonpartisan election

No. of Judges: 7

Terms: 6 years

Method of Retention: Nonpartisan election

PRIMARY ELECTION PROCESS

Presidential
  Type: Caucus/Open
  Date: February 5, 2008
State
  Type: Caucus/Open
  Date: September 14, 2010

STATE CAMPAIGN FINANCE

Contribution Regulations: Individuals are limited to contribution amounts dictated by the candidate office and election year. Bundled contributions are limited to $2,000 in election years and $500 in nonelection years for Governor and Lieutenant Governor candidates; $1,000 in election years and $200 in nonelection years for Attorney General candidates; $500 in election years and $100 in nonelection years for Secretary of State, State Auditor, and State Representatives; $300 in election years and $100 in nonelection years for local government office candidates. Anonymous contributions are limited to $20. Political parties are limited to 10 times the contribution limits imposed on an individual.
Fundraising Limits: Candidates who accept public funding is limited to personal contributions of 10 times the candidate's election year contribution limit.
Online Filing: Yes
Reporting Cycle Dates: Reports must be filed by 15 days before the primary election, 10 days before a general election, 7 days before a special primary and special election, and 10 days after a special election cycle as well as annually by January 31.

LOBBYING GUIDELINES

All lobbyists are required to register within 5 days of being employed and file reports by January 15 and June 15.

BALLOT INITIATIVES AND REFERENDUM

Referendum: No
Ballot Initiative: No
Recall Election: Yes

MISSISSIPPI

STATE VOTER TURNOUT

Population: 2,918,715
Registered Voters
   2000: 1,739,858
   2002: 1,683,928
   2004: 1,469,608
   2006: 1,778,245
   2008: 1,873,740
Turnout
   2000: 47.8% (Highest Office/Voting-Age Pop.): 994,184 / 2,077,117
   2002: 29.2% (Highest Office/Voting-Age Pop.): 615,609 / 2,097,888
   2004: 54.2% (Highest Office/Voting-Age Pop.): 1,152,365 / 2,126,385
   2006: 28.5% (Highest Office/Voting-Age Pop.): 610,921 / 2,139,918
   2008: 57.3% (Highest Office/Voting-Age Pop.): 2,805,986 / 2,179,170
Youth Turnout (18–29 years old)
   2000: 45%
   2002: 21%
   2004: 52%
   2006: 25%
   2008: 57%

STATEWIDE ELECTION OUTCOMES

Presidential Vote 2004: 1,152,145 votes cast
   Bush (R)   54.9%
   Kerry (D)   44.5%
Presidential Vote 2008: 1,289,865 votes cast
   Obama (D)   43.0%
   McCain (R)   56.2%
Gubernatorial Vote 2007: 744,039 votes cast
   Barbour (R)   57.0%
   Eaves (D)   43.0%
Electoral College Votes: 6

VOTING REGULATIONS

Residency Requirements: Resident of city or town for 30 days
Absentee Ballot: Yes
   Criteria: Available for voters absent from county of residence for various reasons or who are 65 years of age or older, disabled, or hospitalized.

Advance Voting: No (absentee in-person voting is available)
Provisional Balloting: Yes
Vote by Phone: No
Registration Deadline: 30 days prior to election
Secretary of State Website: http://www.sos.state.ms.us/elections/elections.asp

CANDIDATE REGULATIONS

Qualifications
   Governor: 30 years old, state resident for 5 years, U.S. citizen for 20 years
   State Senator: 25 years old, district resident for 2 years, state resident for 4 years
   State Representative: 21 years old, district resident for 2 years, state resident for 4 years
Filing Fees
   Governor: $300 (for party candidates)
   State Senate: $15 (for party candidates)
   State House: $15 (for party candidates)
Filing Deadlines
   Presidential Primary: January 14
   Independent/Third Party in Presidential Election: September 5
   Congressional Primary: March 1, 2010
   Independent/Third Party in General Election: March 1, 2010
Online Filing: No
Petition Signature Requirements
   Major Party: President: No requirement
   Minor Party: President: 1,000

JUDICIAL ELECTIONS

Justice Chosen: By district
Method of Selection
   Unexpired Term: Gubernatorial appointment
   Full Term: Nonpartisan election
No. of Judges: 9
Terms: 8 years
Method of Retention: Nonpartisan election

PRIMARY ELECTION PROCESS

Presidential
   Type: Primary/Open
   Date: March 11, 2008
State
   Type: Primary/Open
   Date: June 1, 2010

STATE CAMPAIGN FINANCE

Contribution Regulations: Corporations are limited to $1,000 to any one political party or candidate's entire campaign for any calendar year. Individuals, except state highway patrol members, are not limited to the amount they can contribute.
Fundraising Limits: Candidates are not limited to the amount they are allowed to raise.
Online Filing: Yes
Reporting Cycle Dates: Reports must be filed by the 7th day before any election and every 4th year beginning after 1999, 10 days after May 31, June 30, September 30, and December 31.

LOBBYING GUIDELINES

All lobbyists are required to register within 5 days of being employed and file reports by January 30, February 25, and April 29.

BALLOT INITIATIVES AND REFERENDUM

Referendum: No
Ballot Initiative: Yes
Recall Election: No

MISSOURI

STATE VOTER TURNOUT

Population: 5,878,415
Registered Voters
   2000: 3,860,672
   2002: 3,391,153
   2004: 4,194,416
   2006: 4,007,174
   2008: 4,205,774
Turnout
   2000: 56.2% (Highest Office/Voting-Age Pop.): 2,359,892 / 4,190,591
   2002: 43.9% (Highest Office/Voting-Age Pop.): 1,877,620 / 4,263,174
   2004: 62.9% (Highest Office/Voting-Age Pop.): 2,731,364 / 4,339,916
   2006: 48.1% (Highest Office/Voting-Age Pop.): 2,128,459 / 4,426,278
   2008: 65.0% (Highest Office/Voting-Age Pop.): 2,925,205 / 4,502,320
Youth Turnout (18–29 years old)
   2000: 39%
   2002: 26%
   2004: 52%
   2006: 32%
   2008: 55%

STATEWIDE ELECTION OUTCOMES

Presidential Vote 2004: 2,731,364 votes cast
   Bush (R)   53.3%
   Kerry (D)   46.1%
Presidential Vote 2008: 2,925,205 votes cast
   Obama (D)   49.3%
   McCain (R)   49.4%
Gubernatorial Vote 2008: 2,877,778 votes cast
   Nixon (D)   58.4%
   Hulshof (R)   39.5%
Electoral College Votes: 9

VOTING REGULATIONS

Residency Requirements: Missouri resident
Absentee Ballot: Yes
   Criteria: Available for voters who are absent from election jurisdiction, or due to disability, illness, official election duties, religion, or incar-

ceration. Must be requested by mail or fax by 5:00 p.m. on Wednesday prior to election, or in person by 5:00 p.m. on day prior to election. Ballots must be received by close of polls on day of election.

Advance Voting: Yes

    Criteria: Available through absentee ballot process

Provisional Balloting: Yes

Vote by Phone: No

Registration Deadline: By close of business on the 4th Wednesday prior to election.

Secretary of State Website: http://www.sos.mo.gov/elections/

CANDIDATE REGULATIONS

Qualifications

    Governor: 30 years old, state resident for 10 years, U.S. citizen for 15 years

    State Senator: 30 years old, district resident for 1 year, state resident for 3 years

    State Representative: 24 years old, district resident for 1 year, state resident for 2 years

Filing Fees

    Governor: $200

    State Senate: $50

    State House: $50

Filing Deadlines

    Presidential Primary: November 20

    Independent/Third Party in Presidential Election: July 28, 5:00 p.m.

    Congressional Primary: March 30, 2010

    Independent/Third Party in General Election: August 26, 2010

Online Filing: No

Petition Signature Requirements

    Major Party: President: 37,513 (3% of qualified electors in last general election for Governor)

    Minor Party: 5,000 signatures (qualified electors; valid addresses must appear)

JUDICIAL ELECTIONS

Justice Chosen: At large

Method of Selection

Unexpired Term: Gubernatorial appointment from judicial nominating commission.
Full Term: Gubernatorial appointment from judicial nominating commission.
No. of Judges: 7
Terms: 12 years
Method of Retention: Retention election

PRIMARY ELECTION PROCESS

Presidential
   Type: Primary/Open
   Date: March 5, 2008
State
   Type: Primary/Open
   Date: August 3, 2010

STATE CAMPAIGN FINANCE

Contribution Regulations: Individuals are limited to contributions of $1,175 for Governor, Lieutenant Governor, Secretary of State, State Treasurer, State Auditor, or Attorney General; $575 for State Senator; $300 for State Representative or other office; judicial offices vary with population of the district. Cash contributions are limited to $100 and anonymous contributions limited to $25.
Fundraising Limits: Candidates are not limited to the amount they are allowed to raise.
Online Filing: Yes, required if more than $5,000 is received or spent.
Reporting Cycle Dates: Reports must be filed by the 8th day before an election, 30 days after an election, and the 15th day following the close of each calendar quarter.

LOBBYING GUIDELINES

All lobbyists are required to register within 5 days of being employed paying a registration fee of $10 and file reports monthly on the 10th, electronically with the Missouri Election Commission's web-based system and annually on March 15 and May 30.

BALLOT INITIATIVES AND REFERENDUM

Referendum: Yes
Ballot Initiative: Yes
Recall Election: No

Montana

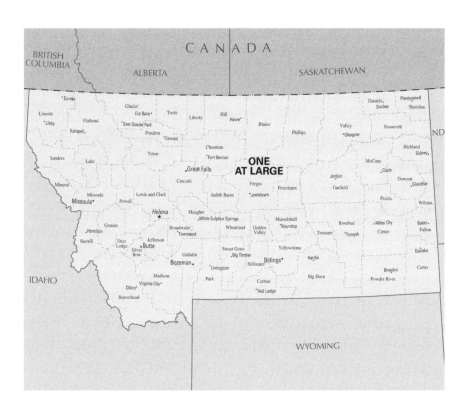

STATE VOTER TURNOUT

Population: 957,681
Registered Voters
  2000: 698,260
  2002: 514,668
  2004: 638,474
  2006: 649,436
  2008: 668,085
Turnout
  2000: 60.6% (Highest Office/Voting-Age Pop.): 410,986 / 675,571
  2002: 47.7% (Highest Office/Voting-Age Pop.): 331,321 / 689,798
  2004: 63.4% (Highest Office/Voting-Age Pop.): 450,445 / 710,024
  2006: 55.6% (Highest Office/Voting-Age Pop.): 406,505 / 731,365
  2008: 65.3% (Highest Office/Voting-Age Pop.): 490,109 / 749,988
Youth Turnout (18–29 years old)
  2000: 42%
  2002: 26%
  2004: 51%
  2006: 39%
  2008: 46%

STATEWIDE ELECTION OUTCOMES

Presidential Vote 2004: 450,434 votes cast
  Bush (R)   59.1%
  Kerry (D)   38.6%
Presidential Vote 2008: 490,109 votes cast
  Obama (D)   47.4%
  McCain (R)   49.5%
Gubernatorial Vote 2008: 2,703,752 votes cast
  Schweitzer (D)   65.5%
  Brown (R)   32.5%
Electoral College Votes: 3

VOTING REGULATIONS

Residency Requirements: County resident for 30 days
Absentee Ballot: Yes
  Criteria: Available for all voters, without excuse. May be requested starting 75 days prior to election and ending 12:00 p.m. on day prior to election. Must be returned by close of polls on day of election.

Advance Voting: Yes
  Criteria: Available through absentee voting.
Provisional Balloting: Yes
Vote by Phone: No
Registration Deadline: 30 days prior to election. Late registration available until day of election.
Secretary of State Website: http://sos.mt.gov/Elections/index.asp

CANDIDATE REGULATIONS

Qualifications
  Governor: 25 years old, state resident for 2 years
  State Senator: 18 years, district resident for 6 months, state resident for 1 year
  State Representative: 18 years, district resident for 6 months, state resident for 1 year
Filing Fees
  Governor: $1,791.27
  State Senate: $15
  State House: $15
Filing Deadlines
  Presidential Primary: March 20
  Independent/Third Party in Presidential Election: August 13
  Congressional Primary: March 15, 2010
  Independent/Third Party in General Election: March 8, 2010
Online Filing: Yes
Petition Signature Requirements
  Major Party: President: 5,000
  Minor Party: President: 5,000

JUDICIAL ELECTIONS

Justice Chosen: At large
Method of Selection
  Unexpired Term: Gubernatorial appointment from judicial nominating commission with consent of the legislature.
  Full Term: Nonpartisan election.
No. of Judges: 7
Terms: 8 years
Method of Retention: Nonpartisan election.

PRIMARY ELECTION PROCESS

Presidential
   Type: Democrats: Primary/Open; Republicans: Caucus/Closed
   Date: February 5, 2008
State
   Type: Primary/Open
   Date: June 8, 2010

STATE CAMPAIGN FINANCE

Contribution Regulations: Individuals are limited to aggregate contributions of $400 for Governor and Lieutenant Governor; $200 for state offices other than Governor and Lieutenant Governor; $100 for any other public office. Political parties are limited to aggregate contributions of $15,000 for Governor and Lieutenant Governor; $5,000 for statewide office; $2,000 for Public Service Commissioner; $800 for State Senate candidates; $500 for candidates of any other public office. Corporations are not permitted to make campaign contributions.
Fundraising Limits: Candidates are not limited to the amount they are allowed to raise.
Online Filing: Yes
Reporting Cycle Dates: Reports must be filed with the Commissioner of Political Practices and report dates can be found on the Montana state website.

LOBBYING GUIDELINES

All lobbyists are required to register within 7 days of being employed and file reports by February 15.

BALLOT INITIATIVES AND REFERENDUM

Referendum: Yes
Ballot Initiative: Yes
Recall Election: Yes

NEBRASKA

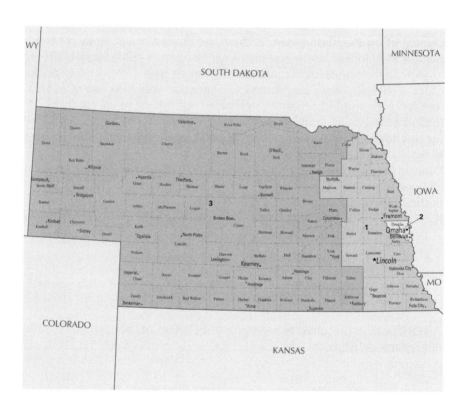

STATE VOTER TURNOUT

Population: 1,783,432
Registered Voters
  2000: 1,085,217
  2002: 1,083,544
  2004: 1,160,193
  2006: 1,138,422
  2008: 1,157,034
Turnout
  2000: 55.0% (Highest Office/Voting-Age Pop.): 696,983 / 1,265,845
  2002: 37.3% (Highest Office/Voting-Age Pop.): 480,991 / 1,282,724
  2004: 59.8% (Highest Office/Voting-Age Pop.): 778,186 / 1,302,049
  2006: 45.1% (Highest Office/Voting-Age Pop.): 596,087 / 1,321,923
  2008: 70.1% (Highest Office/Voting-Age Pop.): 811,823 / 1,157,345
Youth Turnout (18–29 years old)
  2000: Unavailable
  2002: 19%
  2004: 42%
  2006: 27%
  2008: 48%

STATEWIDE ELECTION OUTCOMES

Presidential Vote 2004: 778,186 votes cast
  Bush (R)   65.9%
  Kerry (D)   32.7%
Presidential Vote 2008: 801,281 votes cast
  Obama (D)   41.6%
  McCain (R) 56.5%
Gubernatorial Vote 2006: 593,357 votes cast
  Heineman (R)   73.4%
  Hahn (D)   24.5%
Electoral College Votes: 5

VOTING REGULATIONS

Residency Requirements: Nebraska resident on or before registration deadline
Absentee Ballot: Yes
  Criteria: Considered early voting. Ballots may be requested beginning 120 days prior to election and ending at 4:00 p.m. on Wednesday prior

to election. Ballots may be cast beginning 35 days prior to election and ending by close of polls on day of election.

Advance Voting: Yes
   Criteria: Identical to absentee ballot process.
Provisional Balloting: Yes
Vote by Phone: No
Registration Deadline: 3rd Friday prior to election by mail; 6:00 p.m. on 2nd Friday prior to election in person.
Secretary of State Website: http://www.sos.state.ne.us/dyindex .html#boxingName

CANDIDATE REGULATIONS

Qualifications
   Governor: 30 years old, state resident for 5 years, U.S. citizen for 5 years
   State Senator: 21 years old, district and state resident
Filing Fees
   Governor: $1,050
   State Senate: $120
Filing Deadlines
   Presidential Primary: March 13
   Independent/Third Party in Presidential Election: September 1 (Independent), September 4 (Third Party)
   Congressional Primary: March 1, 2010
   Independent/Third Party in General Election: September 1, 2010
Online Filing: No
Petition Signature Requirements
   Major Party: President: 5,921
   Minor Party: President: 2,500

JUDICIAL ELECTIONS

Justice Chosen: Chief Justice: at large; Associates: by district
Method of Selection
   Unexpired Term: Gubernatorial appointment from judicial nominating commission.
   Full Term: Gubernatorial appointment from judicial nominating commission.
No. of Judges: 7
Terms: 3 years for 1st election, every 6 years thereafter.
Method of Retention: Retention election

PRIMARY ELECTION PROCESS

Presidential
  Type: Caucus/Closed
  Date: Democrats: February 9, 2008; Republicans: July 12, 2008
State
  Type: Caucus/Closed
  Date: May 11, 2010

STATE CAMPAIGN FINANCE

Contribution Regulations: There are no limits on the amount of contributions that may be made by any contributor to a candidate or committee.
Fundraising Limits: The Campaign Finance Limitation Act provides public financing for candidates who agree to abide by statutory spending limitations applicable to the office sought, including candidates for the State Legislature, and, if sufficient funds are available for a given election period, candidates for one or more of the following state offices designated by the Nebraska Accountability and Disclosure Commission according to statutory criteria.
Online Filing: No
Reporting Cycle Dates: By 30th day and 10th day before a primary or general election, and 40th day after primary election, and 70th day after general election. Annual statement due by January 31 for preceding year if statements not required to be filed during previous years. Reports of contributions of $1,000 or more received within 14 days before election is required to be filed within 5 days after receipt.

LOBBYING GUIDELINES

Within 45 days after the end of the legislative session, lobbyists must file a Statement of Activity and then file quarterly lobbying reports due April 30, 2009, July 30, 2009, October 30, 2009, and February 1, 2010.

BALLOT INITIATIVES AND REFERENDUM

Referendum: Yes
Ballot Initiative: Yes
Recall Election: No

Nevada

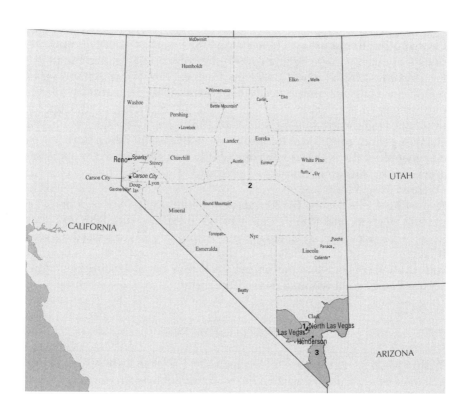

STATE VOTER TURNOUT

Population: 2,600,167
Registered Voters
  2000: 898,347
  2002: 869,801
  2004: 1,073,869
  2006: 991,054
  2008: 1,207,423
Turnout
  2000: 40.2% (Highest Office/Voting-Age Pop.): 608,970 / 1,521,286
  2002: 31.1% (Highest Office/Voting-Age Pop.): 504,079 / 1,630,532
  2004: 47.3% (Highest Office/Voting-Age Pop.): 829,587 / 1,753,843
  2006: 31.1% (Highest Office/Voting-Age Pop.): 582,572 / 1,870,315
  2008: 80.3% (Highest Office/Voting-Age Pop.): 970,019 / 1,207,423
Youth Turnout (18–29 years old)
  2000: Unavailable
  2002: 20%
  2004: 44%
  2006: 20%
  2008: 49%

STATEWIDE ELECTION OUTCOMES

Presidential Vote 2004: 829,587 votes cast
  Bush (R)   50.5%
  Kerry (D)   47.9%
Presidential Vote 2008: 967,848 votes cast
  Obama (D)   55.2%
  McCain (R)   42.7%
Gubernatorial Vote 2006: 582,158 votes cast
  Gibbons (R)   47.9%
  Titus (D)   43.9%
Electoral College Votes: 5

VOTING REGULATIONS

Residency Requirements: Nevada resident for 30 days
Absentee Ballot: Yes

Criteria: Available for all voters unable to be at polls on day of election. Must be requested 7 days prior to election and returned by 7:00 p.m. on day of election.
Advance Voting: Yes
    Criteria: Dates and times vary by county.
Provisional Balloting: Yes
Vote by Phone: No
Registration Deadline: 31 days prior to election by mail or at Department of Motor Vehicles; 21 days prior to election at county clerk's office.
Secretary of State Website: http://sos.state.nv.us/

CANDIDATE REGULATIONS

Qualifications
    Governor: 25 years old, state resident for 2 years
    State Senator: 18 years old, district resident
    State Representative: 18 years old, district resident
Filing Fees
    Governor: $300
    State Senate: $100
    State House: $100
Filing Deadlines
    Presidential Primary: n/a (Caucus on January 19)
    Independent/Third Party in Presidential Election: April 11
    Congressional Primary: March 12, 2010
    Independent/Third Party in General Election: February 4, 2010
Online Filing: No
Petition Signature Requirements
    Major Party: President: 5,746 (1% of the votes cast during the last elections for U.S. Representative)
    Minor Party: President: 5,746 (1% of the votes cast during the last elections for U.S. Representative)

JUDICIAL ELECTIONS

Justice Chosen: At large
Method of Selection
    Unexpired Term: Gubernatorial appointment from judicial nominating commission.
    Full Term: Nonpartisan election.

No. of Judges: 7
Terms: 6 years
Method of Retention: Nonpartisan election.

PRIMARY ELECTION PROCESS

Presidential
    Type: Caucus/Closed
    Date: January 19, 2008
State
    Type: Caucus/Open
    Date: June 8, 2010

STATE CAMPAIGN FINANCE

Contribution Regulations: Contributions to a candidate for any office (except a federal office) by any person, natural or otherwise, may not exceed $5,000 for the primary election or primary city election and $5,000 for the general election or general city election.
Fundraising Limits: Candidates are not limited to the amount they are allowed to raise.
Online Filing: Yes
Reporting Cycle Dates: Reports are due 7 days before primary, 7 days before general election, and 15th day of 2nd month after general election.

LOBBYING GUIDELINES

Lobbyists must register and pay $120 but the fee is only $20 for nonpaid lobbyists. Monthly expenditure reports are due on March 10 (for February), April 10 (for March), May 11 (for April), June 10 (for May), and July 11 (for June).

BALLOT INITIATIVES AND REFERENDUM

Referendum: Yes
Ballot Initiative: Yes
Recall Election: Yes

New Hampshire

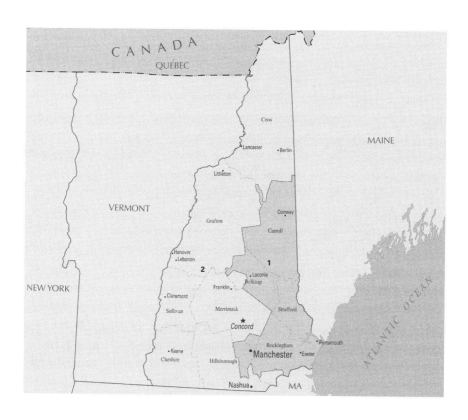

STATE VOTER TURNOUT

Population: 1,315,828
Registered Voters
   2000: 856,519
   2002: 690,159
   2004: 855,861
   2006: 848,317
   2008: 865,746
Turnout
   2000: 60.7% (Highest Office/Voting-Age Pop.): 569,081 / 935,466
   2002: 46.0% (Highest Office/Voting-Age Pop.): 447,135 / 964,299
   2004: 68.4% (Highest Office/Voting-Age Pop.): 677,738 / 990,260
   2006: 39.9% (Highest Office/Voting-Age Pop.): 403,531 / 1,012,033
   2008: 69.4% (Highest Office/Voting-Age Pop.): 710,970 / 1,024,054
Youth Turnout (18–29 years old)
   2000: 46%
   2002: 24%
   2004: 58%
   2006: 19%
   2008: 62%

STATEWIDE ELECTION OUTCOMES

Presidential Vote 2004: 677,738 votes cast
   Bush (R)   48.9%
   Kerry (D)   50.2%
Presidential Vote 2008: 710,970 votes cast
   Obama (D)   54.1%
   McCain (R) 44.5%
Gubernatorial Vote 2006: 403,679 votes cast
   Lynch (D)   74.0%
   Coburn (R) 25.8%
Electoral College Votes: 4

VOTING REGULATIONS

Residency Requirements: New Hampshire resident
Absentee Ballot: Yes
   Criteria: Available for voters absent from polls due to temporary absence, religious beliefs, military service, or physical disability. Available

beginning 30 days prior to election. Must be returned by 5:00 p.m. on day prior to election in person or 5:00 p.m. on day of election by mail.
Advance Voting: No
Provisional Balloting: No
Vote by Phone: Yes
Registration Deadline: 10 days prior to election or in person before 5:00 p.m. on day of election.
Secretary of State Website: http://www.sos.nh.gov/electionsnew.html

CANDIDATE REGULATIONS

Qualifications
  Governor: 30 years old, state resident for 7 years
  State Senator: 30 years old, district resident, state resident for 7 years
  State Representative: 18 years old, town/ward resident, state resident for 2 years
Filing Fees
  Governor: $100
  State Senate: $10
  State House: $2
Filing Deadlines
  Presidential Primary: November 2
  Independent/Third Party in Presidential Election: September 3
  Congressional Primary: June 11, 2010
  Independent/Third Party in General Election: September 1, 2010
Online Filing: No
Petition Signature Requirements
  Major Party: President: 12,524
  Minor Party: President: 3,000 (1,500 from each congressional district)

JUDICIAL ELECTIONS

Justice Chosen: At large
Method of Selection
  Unexpired Term: Gubernatorial appointment with approval of elected Executive Council
  Full Term: Gubernatorial appointment with approval of elected Executive Council
No. of Judges: 5
Terms: 5 years
Method of Retention: Good behavior

PRIMARY ELECTION PROCESS

Presidential
   Type: Primary/Open
   Date: January 8, 2008
State
   Type: Primary/Open
   Date: September 14, 2010

STATE CAMPAIGN FINANCE

Contribution Regulations: The maximum limit for contributions that may be made by any person, including a corporation, to a candidate (except by the candidate), a political committee, or a political party is $5,000 per primary or general election. Candidates may voluntarily agree to limit expenditure amounts. A labor union or partnership is prohibited by statute from making political contributions.

A candidate for state executive, state legislative, or county office whose expenditures exceed $500 and a political committee whose receipts or expenditures in support of a candidate, ballot measure, or political party exceed $500 must file periodic statements of receipts and expenditures with the Secretary of State. A political committee is required to file a statement of independent expenditures with the Secretary of State each time independent expenditures exceeding $500 are made. All nonparty political committees are required to register with the Secretary of State no later than 24 hours after receiving any contribution in excess of $500 or before making any expenditure in excess of $500.

Fundraising Limits: Gubernatorial and U.S. senatorial candidates limited to spending no more than $625 per election. U.S. representative candidates limited to spending no more than $350,000 per election. Candidates for state senate are limited to spending no more than $20,000 per election and state representative and county office candidates limited to spending no more than 50 cents per registered voter per election.

Online Filing: Yes

Reporting Cycle Dates: Due Wednesday 12 weeks before primary (except political committee of candidate or political party), Wednesday 3 weeks before election, and 2nd Wednesday after election. Every 6 months after election until obligations satisfied or surplus depleted. Notice of a contribution greater than $500 received after second Wednesday before election is to be filed within 24 hours. Political committee report of independent expenditures to be filed within 24 hours after aggregate expenditures greater than $500 are made and thereafter each time $500 more is spent.

LOBBYING GUIDELINES

Each lobbyist shall file with the Secretary of State itemized statements under oath of all fees received from any lobbying client that are related, directly or indirectly, to lobbying, such as public advocacy, government relations, or public relations services including research, monitoring legislation, and related legal work. Statements shall be filed no later than the 2nd Friday of each month. A separate monthly statement shall be filed by a lobbyist for each client for whom there has been reportable transactions.

BALLOT INITIATIVES AND REFERENDUM

Referendum: No
Ballot Initiative: No
Recall Election: No

New Jersey

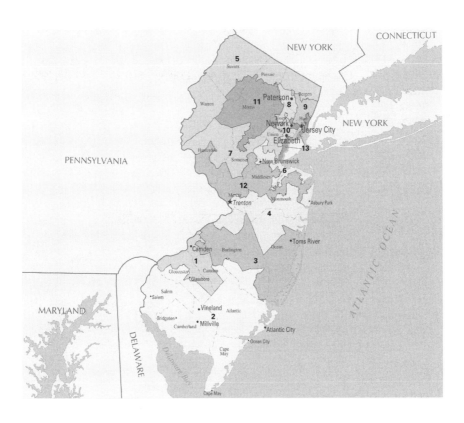

STATE VOTER TURNOUT

Population: 8,685,920
Registered Voters
  2000: 4,710,768
  2002: 4,194,089
  2004: 5,011,693
  2006: 4,848,956
  2008: 5,351,669
Turnout
  2000: 50.1% (Highest Office/Voting-Age Pop.): 3,187,226 / 6,363,533
  2002: 32.6% (Highest Office/Voting-Age Pop.): 2,112,604 / 6,469,352
  2004: 55.2% (Highest Office/Voting-Age Pop.): 3,611,691 / 6,542,049
  2006: 34.1% (Highest Office/Voting-Age Pop.): 2,250,070 / 6,598,368
  2008: 58.3% (Highest Office/Voting-Age Pop.): 3,868,237 / 6,639,395
Youth Turnout (18–29 years old)
  2000: 41%
  2002: 17%
  2004: 51%
  2006: 22%
  2008: 53%

STATEWIDE ELECTION OUTCOMES

Presidential Vote 2004: 3,611,691 votes cast
  Bush (R)   46.2%
  Kerry (D)   52.9%
Presidential Vote 2008: 3,868,237 votes cast
  Obama (D)   57.3%
  McCain (R)   41.7%
Gubernatorial Vote 2008: 2,290,099 votes cast
  Corzine (D)   53.5%
  Forrester (R)   43.0%
Electoral College Votes: 15

VOTING REGULATIONS

Residency Requirements: County resident for 30 days
Absentee Ballot: Yes
  Criteria: Available for all voters; no excuse is necessary. Must be requested
  by 7 days prior to election by mail or 3:00 p.m. on day prior to election in
  person. Must be returned by close of polls on day of election.

Advance Voting: Yes
  Criteria: Available through absentee voting process.
Provisional Balloting: Yes
Vote by Phone: No
Registration Deadline: 21 days prior to election
Secretary of State Website: http://www.njelections.org/

CANDIDATE REGULATIONS

Qualifications
  Governor: 30 years old, state resident for 7 years, natural-born U.S. citizen for 20 years
  State Senator: 30 years old, state resident for 4 years
  State Representative: 21 years old, state resident for 2 years
Filing Fees
  Governor: $0
  State Senate: $0
  State House: $0
Filing Deadlines
  Presidential Primary: December 10
  Independent/Third Party in Presidential Election: July 28
  Congressional Primary: April 12, 2010
  Independent/Third Party in General Election: June 8, 2010
Online Filing: No
Petition Signature Requirements
  Major Party: President: No requirement
  Minor Party: President: 800

JUDICIAL ELECTIONS

Justice Chosen: At large
Method of Selection
  Unexpired Term: Gubernatorial appointment with consent of the legislature
  Full Term: Gubernatorial appointment with approval of elected executive council
No. of Judges: 7
Terms: 7 years, then must obtain tenure by generational reappointment and consent by the Senate. Mandatory reappointment at age 70.
Method of Retention: Gubernatorial appointment with approval of elected executive council.

PRIMARY ELECTION PROCESS

Presidential
  Type: Democrats: Primary/Closed; Republicans: Primary/Semiclosed
  Date: February 5, 2008
State
  Type: Democrats; Primary/Closed; Republicans; Primary/Semiclosed
  Date: June 8, 2010

STATE CAMPAIGN FINANCE

Contribution Regulations: Contributions may not exceed maximum amounts set for contributors or recipients. In nongubernatorial campaigns, individuals (other than candidates), corporations, labor organizations, and other groups are limited to $2,200 per each candidate per election; candidates, political committees, and continuing political committees are limited to $7,200 per each candidate and political committee per election.
Fundraising Limits: Contribution and solicitation limits may be found on the website for the New Jersey Secretary of State.
Online Filing: No
Reporting Cycle Dates: Candidates, joint candidates committees, and political committees: 29th day and 11th day before election and 20th day after election. If exempted from periodic reporting, file contributions report on scheduled date if aggregate contribution of more than $400 received.

LOBBYING GUIDELINES

All lobbyists are required to register within 30 of accepting a client or after 20 hours of lobbying activity. Lobbyists must also file quarterly lobbying reports.

BALLOT INITIATIVES AND REFERENDUM

Referendum: No
Ballot Initiative: No
Recall Election: Yes

New Mexico

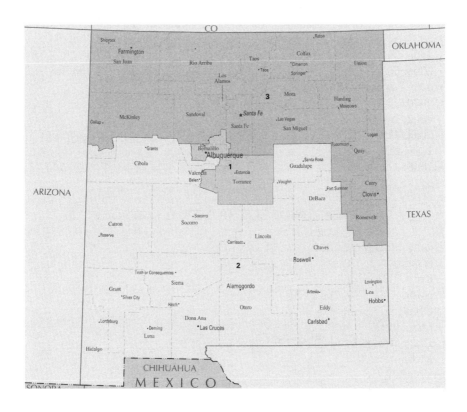

STATE VOTER TURNOUT

Population: 1,969,915
Registered Voters
  2000: 972,895
  2002: 839,592
  2004: 505,356
  2006: 1,088,977
  2008: 1,184,536
Turnout
  2000: 45.4% (Highest Office/Voting-Age Pop.): 598,605 / 1,318,425
  2002: 35.7% (Highest Office/Voting-Age Pop.): 484,229 / 1,358,655
  2004: 53.9% (Highest Office/Voting-Age Pop.): 756,304 / 1,404,259
  2006: 28.6% (Highest Office/Voting-Age Pop.): 561,084 / 1,452,962
  2008: 56.1% (Highest Office/Voting-Age Pop.): 833,365 / 1,485,995
Youth Turnout (18–29 years old)
  2000: 28%
  2002: 16%
  2004: 42%
  2006: 25%
  2008: 47%

STATEWIDE ELECTION OUTCOMES

Presidential Vote 2004: 775,301 votes cast
  Bush (R)   49.8%
  Kerry (D)   49.0%
Presidential Vote 2008: 830,158 votes cast
  Obama (D)   56.9%
  McCain (R)   41.8%
Gubernatorial Vote 2006: 559,170 votes cast
  Richardson (D)   68.8%
  Dendahl (R)   31.2%
Electoral College Votes: 5

VOTING REGULATIONS

Residency Requirements: New Mexico resident
Absentee Ballot: Yes
  Criteria: Available for all voters; no excuse is necessary. Must be requested by 5:00 p.m. on Friday prior to election. Must be returned by
  7:00 p.m. on day of election.

Advance Voting: Yes
   Criteria: Early in-person voting begins 3rd Saturday prior to election and ends the Saturday prior to election.
Provisional Balloting: Yes
Vote by Phone: No
Registration Deadline: 28 days prior to election or Friday after close of registration if in person.
Secretary of State Website: http://www.sos.state.nm.us/sos-elections. html

CANDIDATE REGULATIONS

Qualifications
   Governor: 30 years old, state resident for 5 years
   State Senator: 25 years old, district resident
   State Representative: 21 years old, district resident
Filing Fees
   Governor: $0
   State Senate: $0
   State House: $0
Filing Deadlines
   Presidential Primary: March 14
   Independent/Third Party in Presidential Election: June 4 (Independent); June 24 (Third Party)
   Congressional Primary: February 9, 2010
   Independent/Third Party in General Election: June 2, 2010 (Independent); June 22, 2010 (Third Party)
Online Filing: Yes
Petition Signature Requirements
   Major Party: President: 2,794
   Minor Party: President: 16,764

JUDICIAL ELECTIONS

Justice Chosen: At large
Method of Selection
   Unexpired Term: Gubernatorial appointment from judicial nominating commission
   Full Term: Partisan election
No. of Judges: 5
Terms: 8 years
Method of Retention: Retention election

PRIMARY ELECTION PROCESS

Presidential
  Type: Democrats: Caucus/Closed; Republicans: Primary/Closed
  Date: Democrats: February 5, 2008; Republicans: June 3, 2008
State
  Type: Democrats: Caucus/Closed; Republicans: Primary/Closed
  Date: June 6, 2010

STATE CAMPAIGN FINANCE

Contribution Regulations: New Mexico requires public officials, candidates or their campaign committees, and political committees to file preelection and postelection reports of contributions and expenditures; however, a candidate who files a statement that anticipated receipts or expenditures for a primary or general election will be less than $2,500 for a statewide office is exempted from reporting.
Fundraising Limits: Candidates are not limited to the amount they are allowed to raise.
Online Filing: No
Reporting Cycle Dates: All public officials and candidates—due annually the 2nd Monday in May.

LOBBYING GUIDELINES

Lobbyists must file reports of expenditures and political contributions every January 15 and May 1. In addition they must file within 48 hours for each separate expenditure made or incurred during a legislative session or special sessions that was for $500 or more.

BALLOT INITIATIVES AND REFERENDUM

Referendum: Yes
Ballot Initiative: No
Recall Election: No

NEW YORK

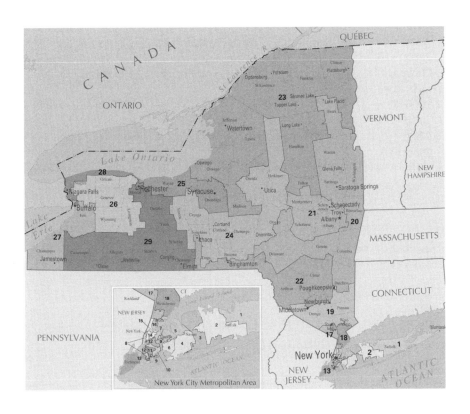

STATE VOTER TURNOUT

Population: 19,297,729
Registered Voters
    2000: 11,262,816
    2002: 10,180,636
    2004: 11,837,068
    2006: 11,669,573
    2008: 12,031,312
Turnout
    2000: 47.5% (Highest Office/Voting-Age Pop.): 6,821,999 / 14,349,129
    2002: 31.4% (Highest Office/Voting-Age Pop.): 4,579,078 / 14,538,422
    2004: 50.2% (Highest Office/Voting-Age Pop.): 7,391,249 / 14,709,398
    2006: 30.3% (Highest Office/Voting-Age Pop.): 4,490,053 / 14,838,076
    2008: 51.0% (Highest Office/Voting-Age Pop.): 7,721,718 / 15,148,270
Youth Turnout (18–29 years old)
    2000: 42%
    2002: 18%
    2004: 45%
    2006: 19%
    2008: 47%

STATEWIDE ELECTION OUTCOMES

Presidential Vote 2004: 7,448,266 votes cast
    Bush (R)   57.9%
    Kerry (D)   39.8%
Presidential Vote 2008: 7,721,718 votes cast
    Obama (D)   62.2%
    McCain (R)   35.6%
Gubernatorial Vote 2006: 4,697,867 votes cast
    Spitzer (D)   65.7%
    Faso (R)   27.1%
Electoral College Votes: 31

VOTING REGULATIONS

Residency Requirements: Resident at current in-state address for 30 days
Absentee Ballot: Yes
    Criteria: Available for voters absent from polls due to illness, disability, unavoidable absence, or incarceration. May be requested starting

30 days prior to election and ending 7 days prior to election. Must be returned by mail postmarked by day prior to election and must reach board of elections no more than 7 days after election.

Advance Voting: Yes

Criteria: In person absentee voting begins at least 32 days prior to election. Available weekdays from 9:00 a.m. to 5:00 p.m. and on weekend prior to election.

Provisional Balloting: Yes

Vote by Phone: No

Registration Deadline: 25 days prior to election

Secretary of State Website: http://www.elections.state.ny.us/

CANDIDATE REGULATIONS

Qualifications

Governor: 30 years old, state resident for 5 years

State Senator: 18 years old, district resident for 1 year, state resident for 5 years

State Representative: 18 years old, district resident for 1 year, state resident for 5 years

Filing Fees:

Governor: $0

State Senate: $0

State House: $0

Filing Deadlines

Presidential Primary: December 6

Independent/Third Party in Presidential Election: August 19

Congressional Primary: July 25, 2010, 12:00 p.m.

Independent/Third Party in General Election: February 3, 2010, 12:00 p.m.

Online Filing: No

Petition Signature Requirements

Major Party: President: No requirement

Minor Party: President: 15,000

JUDICIAL ELECTIONS

Justice Chosen: At large

Method of Selection

Unexpired Term: Gubernatorial appointment from judicial nominating commission with consent of the legislature

Full Term: Gubernatorial appointment from judicial nominating commission with consent of the legislature

No. of Judges: 7

Terms: 14 years

Method of Retention: Gubernatorial appointment from judicial nominating commission with consent of the legislature

PRIMARY ELECTION PROCESS

Presidential
   Type: Primary/Closed
   Date: February 5, 2008
State
   Type: Primary/Closed
   Date: September 14, 2010

STATE CAMPAIGN FINANCE

Contribution Regulations: There are maximum aggregate contribution amounts that may be made to and accepted by a candidate or political committee aiding a candidate in connection with a primary, general, or special election, subject to numerous exemptions for certain "contributors." Individuals, other than a candidate's family, are limited to a total of $150,000 for contributions in candidate-related elections in a calendar year and are also subject to specific limitations for various offices and positions.

Fundraising Limits: No individual, except as may otherwise be provided for a candidate and a candidate's family, may contribute, loan, or guarantee over $150,000 in connection with the nomination or election of persons to state and local public offices and party positions in any one calendar year.

Online Filing: No

Reporting Cycle Dates: General election: 32nd day and 11th day before and 27th day after the election. Periodic statements are also required by January 15 and July 15 in each subsequent year until activities terminated.

LOBBYING GUIDELINES

All lobbyists are required to file a biennial statement when they are compensated in excess of $5,000. These statements must be filed before

January 1 of the biennial period. Reports include names and addresses of lobbyists, the organizational affiliation or client, and the issues lobbied.

BALLOT INITIATIVES AND REFERENDUM

Referendum: No
Ballot Initiative: No
Recall Election: No

NORTH CAROLINA

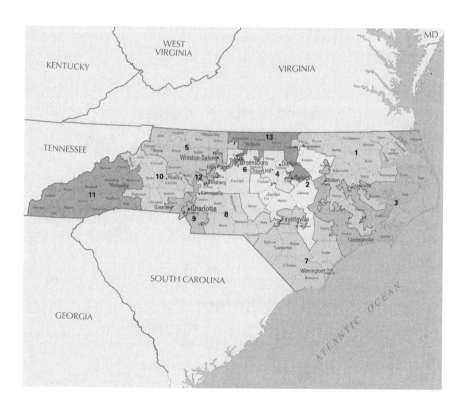

STATE VOTER TURNOUT

Population: 9,061,032
Registered Voters
  2000: 5,122,123
  2002: 5,038,826
  2004: 5,526,981
  2006: 5,567,424
  2008: 6,233,330
Turnout
  2000: 47.5% (Highest Office/Voting-Age Pop.): 2,911,262 / 6,140,577
  2002: 37.2% (Highest Office/Voting-Age Pop.): 2,331,181 / 6,310,783
  2004: 53.9% (Highest Office/Voting-Age Pop.): 3,501,007 / 6,490,833
  2006: 28.7% (Highest Office/Voting-Age Pop.): 1,940,808 / 6,752,018
  2008: 62.0% (Highest Office/Voting-Age Pop.): 4,353,739 / 7,023,865
Youth Turnout (18–29 years old)
  2000: 40%
  2002: 18%
  2004: 45%
  2006: 21%
  2008: 55%

STATEWIDE ELECTION OUTCOMES

Presidential Vote 2004: 3,501,007 votes cast
  Bush (R)   56.0%
  Kerry (D)   43.6%
Presidential Vote 2008: 4,310,789 votes cast
  Obama (D)   49.7%
  McCain (R)   49.4%
Gubernatorial Vote 2008: 4,268,941 votes cast
  Perdue (D)   50.3%
  McCrory (R)   46.9%
Electoral College Votes: 15

VOTING REGULATIONS

Residency Requirements: State and county resident for 30 days
Absentee Ballot: Yes
  Criteria: Available to all voters; no excuse is necessary. Must be requested by 5:00 p.m. on last Tuesday prior to election. May be returned

starting 3rd Thursday prior to election and ending Saturday prior to election.

Advance Voting: Yes

Criteria: In person absentee voting available during absentee voting period (between 3rd Thursday prior to election and Saturday prior to election).

Provisional Balloting: Yes

Vote by Phone: No

Registration Deadline: 5:00 p.m. 25 days prior to election or both registration and voting available during early voting period from 3rd Thursday prior to election to Saturday prior to election.

Secretary of State Website: http://www.sboe.state.nc.us/

CANDIDATE REGULATIONS

Qualifications
   Governor: 30 years old, state resident for 2 years, U.S. citizen for 5 years
   State Senator: 25 years old, district resident for 1 year, state resident for 2 years
   State Representative: 21 years old, district resident for 1 year, state resident
Filing Fees
   Governor: $1,359 (1% of annual salary)
   State Senate: $207 (1% of annual salary)
   State House: $207 (1% of annual salary)
Filing Deadlines
   Presidential Primary: n/a (Caucus on May 6)
   Independent/Third Party in Presidential Election: June 1 (Third party); June 27 (Independent)
   Congressional Primary: February 26, 2010
   Independent/Third Party in General Election: June 25, 2010 (Independent); August 1, 2010 (Third Party)
Online Filing: No
Petition Signature Requirements
   Major Party: President: 86,216 (2% of total number of voters in last gubernatorial election)
   Minor Party: President: 86,216 (2% of total number of voters in last gubernatorial election)

JUDICIAL ELECTIONS

Justice Chosen: At large
Method of Selection
  Unexpired Term: Gubernatorial appointment
  Full Term: Nonpartisan election
No. of Judges: 7
Terms: 8 years
Method of Retention: Nonpartisan election

PRIMARY ELECTION PROCESS

Presidential
  Type: Primary/Semiclosed
  Date: May 6, 2008
State
  Type: Primary/Semiclosed
  Date: May 4, 2010

STATE CAMPAIGN FINANCE

Contribution Regulations: North Carolina has set a maximum limit of $4,000 for contributions by individuals, nonparty political committees, and other entities to candidates and nonparty political committees in an election. Contributions by corporations and other organizations are prohibited (with some exceptions); however, the officials and members of these organizations may establish a separate segregated fund to be used for political purposes.
Fundraising Limits: Candidates are not limited to the amount which they are allowed to raise.
Online Filing: No
Reporting Cycle Dates: For all candidates and committees, organizational reports are due within 10 days of filing of candidacy or organization of committee.

LOBBYING GUIDELINES

Lobbyists are prohibited from making campaign contributions and may not give gifts to legislators. They also must disclose who they are to the person(s) being lobbied.

BALLOT INITIATIVES AND REFERENDUM

Referendum: No
Ballot Initiative: No
Recall Election: No

North Dakota

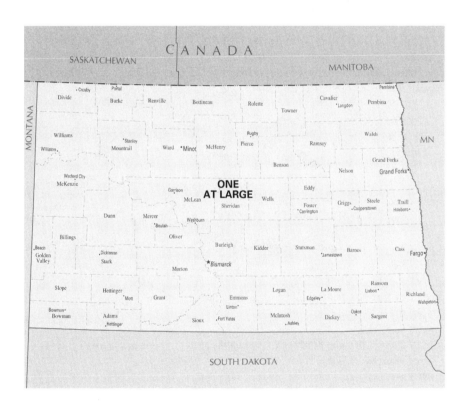

STATE VOTER TURNOUT

Population: 639,715
Registered Voters
  2000: no registration needed
  2002: no registration needed
  2004: no registration needed
  2006: no registration needed
  2008: no registration needed
Turnout
  2000: 59.7% (Highest Office/Voting-Age Pop.): 288,256 / 481,070
  2002: 47.6% (Highest Office/Voting-Age Pop.): 231,030 / 482,721
  2004: 63.8% (Highest Office/Voting-Age Pop.): 312,833 / 490,218
  2006: 44.1% (Highest Office/Voting-Age Pop.): 218,152 / 494,923
  2008: 64.6% (Highest Office/Voting-Age Pop.): 321,133 / 496,906
Youth Turnout (18–29 years old)
  2000: 61%
  2002: 33%
  2004: 56%
  2006: 30%
  2008: 57%

STATEWIDE ELECTION OUTCOMES

Presidential Vote 2004: 312,833 votes cast
  Bush (R)   62.9%
  Kerry (D)   35.5%
Presidential Vote 2008: 316,621 votes cast
  Obama (D)   44.6%
  McCain (R)   53.2%
Gubernatorial Vote 2008: 315,692 votes cast
  Hoeven (R)   74.4%
  Mathern (D)   23.5%
Electoral College Votes: 3

VOTING REGULATIONS

Residency Requirements: North Dakota resident; precinct resident for 30 days
Absentee Ballot: Yes

Criteria: Available for all voters beginning 40 days prior to election. Must be returned by day prior to election.
Advance Voting: Yes
  Criteria: No excuse is required. Dates and times vary by county.
Provisional Balloting: No
Vote by Phone: No
Registration Deadline: No registration is required.
Secretary of State Website: http://www.nd.gov/sos/electvote/

CANDIDATE REGULATIONS

Qualifications
  Governor: 30 years old, state resident for 5 years
  State Senator: 18 years old, district resident, state resident for 1 year
  State Representative: 18 years old, district resident, state resident for 1 year
Filing Fees
  Governor: $0
  State Senate: $0
  State House: $0
Filing Deadlines
  Presidential Primary: n/a (Caucus on February 5)
  Independent/Third Party in Presidential Election: September 5, 4:00 p.m.
  Congressional Primary: April 9, 2010, 4:00 p.m.
  Independent/Third Party in General Election: September 3, 2010, 4:00 p.m.
Online Filing: No
Petition Signature Requirements
  Major Party: President: 7,000
  Minor Party: President: 4,000

JUDICIAL ELECTIONS

Justice Chosen: At large
Method of Selection
  Unexpired Term: Gubernatorial appointment from judicial nominating commission. The governor may appoint from a list of names or call of special election at his discretion.
  Full Term: Nonpartisan election
No. of Judges: 5

Terms: 10 years
Method of Retention: Nonpartisan election

PRIMARY ELECTION PROCESS

Presidential
   Type: Caucus/Open
   Date: February 5, 2008
State
   Type: Caucus/Open
   Date: September 18, 2010

STATE CAMPAIGN FINANCE

Contribution Regulations: A corporation, cooperative operation, limited liability company, or association may not make direct contributions or expenditures other than for the passage or defeat of ballot measures or to promote a general political philosophy, but may form a political committee to establish and administer a separate segregated fund for political purposes.
Fundraising Limits: Candidates are not limited to the amount which they are allowed to raise.
Online Filing: No
Reporting Cycle Dates: Preelection statement is due the 12th day before the election. Year end statement is due January 31 of the following year. Supplemental statement for contribution of $500 or more received in 20-day period before an election must be filed within 48 hours by statewide or legislative office candidate and by referendum/initiative group or person.

LOBBYING GUIDELINES

Each registered lobbyist must file with the Secretary of State a detailed expenditure report on or before August 1, following the expiration of the registration period. The Lobbyist Expenditure Report must include a statement as to each expenditure, if any, of $60 or more expended on any single occasion on any individual, including the spouse or other family member or a member of the Legislative Assembly or the Governor, in carrying out the lobbyist's work or include a statement that no reportable expenditures were made during the reporting period.

BALLOT INITIATIVES AND REFERENDUM

Referendum: Yes
Ballot Initiative: Yes
Recall Election: Yes

Ohio

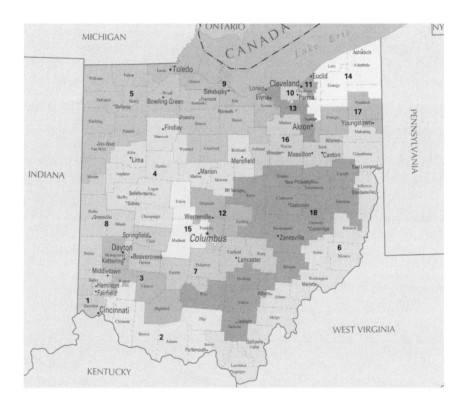

STATE VOTER TURNOUT

Population: 11,466,917
Registered Voters
  2000: 7,537,822
  2002: 7,110,901
  2004: 7,965,110
  2006: 7,860,052
  2008: 8,287,665
Turnout
  2000: 55.4% (Highest Office/Voting-Age Pop.): 4,705,457 / 8,491,722
  2002: 37.6% (Highest Office/Voting-Age Pop.): 3,228,992 / 8,570,838
  2004: 65.1% (Highest Office/Voting-Age Pop.): 5,627,908 / 8,643,995
  2006: 46.3% (Highest Office/Voting-Age Pop.): 4,022,754 / 8,697,456
  2008: 65.3% (Highest Office/Voting-Age Pop.): 5,775,369 / 8,769,030
Youth Turnout (18–29 years old)
  2000: 41%
  2002: 21%
  2004: 54%
  2006: 31%
  2008: 55%

STATEWIDE ELECTION OUTCOMES

Presidential Vote 2004: 5,627,908 votes cast
  Bush (R)   50.8%
  Kerry (D)   48.7%
Presidential Vote 2008: 5,698,260 votes cast
  Obama (D)   51.5%
  McCain (R)   46.9%
Gubernatorial Vote 2006: 4,022,928 votes cast
  Strickland (D)   60.5%
  Blackwell (R)   36.7%
Electoral College Votes: 20

VOTING REGULATIONS

Residency Requirements: Ohio resident for 30 days
Absentee Ballot: Yes
  Criteria: Available for all voters; no excuse is necessary. Must be requested by 12:00 p.m. on Saturday prior to election by mail or fax, or by

day before election in person. May be returned beginning 35 days prior to election and ending 7:30 p.m. on day of election. May be returned no later than 10 days after election if mailed from out of the country.
Advance Voting: Yes
   Criteria: Available as in person absentee voting beginning 35 days prior to election and ending at close of business hours on day prior to election.
Provisional Balloting: Yes
Vote by Phone: No
Registration Deadline: 30 days prior to election
Secretary of State Website: http://www.sos.state.oh.us/

CANDIDATE REGULATIONS

Qualifications
   Governor: 18 years, state resident (qualified elector)
   State Senator: 18 years, district resident for 1 year
   State Representative: 18 years, district resident for 1 year
Filing Fees
   Governor: $150
   State Senate: $85
   State House: $85
Filing Deadlines
   Presidential Primary: January 4
   Independent/Third Party in Presidential Election: August 21 (Independent)
   Congressional Primary: February 18, 2010
   Independent/Third Party in General Election: February 18, 2010 (Third Party); May 3, 2010 (Independent)
Online Filing: No
Petition Signature Requirements
   Major Party: President: No requirement
   Minor Party: President: 5,000

JUDICIAL ELECTIONS

Justice Chosen: At large
Method of Selection
   Unexpired Term: Gubernatorial appointment
   Full Term: Partisan election during primary process. Party affiliation is not included on ballot during general election.

No. of Judges: 7
Terms: 6 years
Method of Retention: Partisan election during primary process. Party af-filiation is not included on ballot during general election

PRIMARY ELECTION PROCESS

Presidential
   Type: Primary/Closed
   Date: March 4, 2008
State
   Type: Primary/Closed
   Date: March 2, 2010

STATE CAMPAIGN FINANCE

Contribution Regulations: Each taxpayer may designate that $1 ($2 if a joint return is filed) of the taxpayer's income tax liability be paid for the use of major political parties.
Fundraising Limits: A contribution or contributions aggregating more than $2,500 by an individual may not be made or accepted.
Online Filing: Yes
Reporting Cycle Dates: Reports due the 12th day before and 38th day after an election; annual statement on the last business day of January except in year post-general election statement is filed.

LOBBYING GUIDELINES

Lobbyists must register and then file reports every four months detailing expenditures (spent on legislators) above $50 for food and above $25 for gifts.

BALLOT INITIATIVES AND REFERENDUM

Referendum: Yes
Ballot Initiative: Yes
Recall Election: No

OKLAHOMA

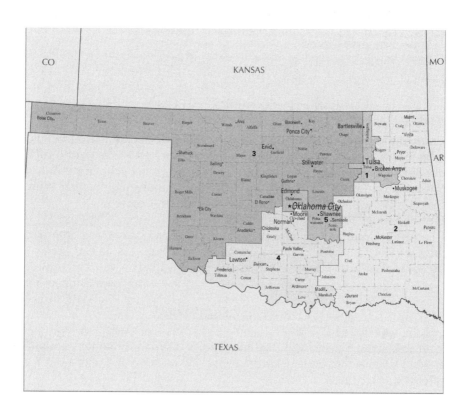

STATE VOTER TURNOUT

Population: 3,617,316
Registered Voters
   2000: 2,233,602
   2002: 1,687,477
   2004: 2,143,978
   2006: 2,075,561
   2008: 2,184,092
Turnout
   2000: 60.6% (Highest Office/Voting-Age Pop.): 410,986 / 675,571
   2002: 47.7% (Highest Office/Voting-Age Pop.): 331,321 / 689,798
   2004: 63.4% (Highest Office/Voting-Age Pop.): 450,445 / 710,024
   2006: 55.6% (Highest Office/Voting-Age Pop.): 406,505 / 731,365
   2008: 65.3% (Highest Office/Voting-Age Pop.): 490,109 / 749,988
Youth Turnout (18–29 years old)
   2000: 42%
   2002: 26%
   2004: 51%
   2006: 39%
   2008: 48%

STATEWIDE ELECTION OUTCOMES

Presidential Vote 2004: 1,463,758 votes cast
   Bush (R)   65.6%
   Kerry (D)   34.4%
Presidential Vote 2008: 1,462,661 votes cast
   Obama (D)   34.4%
   McCain (R)   65.7%
Gubernatorial Vote 2006: 926,462 votes cast
   Henry (D)   66.5%
   Istook (R)   33.5%
Electoral College Votes: 7

VOTING REGULATIONS

Residency Requirements: Oklahoma resident
Absentee Ballot: Yes

Criteria: Available for all voters; no excuse is necessary. Must be requested by 5:00 p.m. on Wednesday prior to election. Must be returned by 7:00 p.m. on day of election.

Advance Voting: Yes
  Criteria: Available as in person absentee voting between 8:00 a.m. and 6:00 p.m. on Friday and Monday prior to election.
Provisional Balloting: Yes
Vote by Phone: Yes
Registration Deadline: 24 days prior to election
Secretary of State Website: http://www.state.ok.us/~elections/

CANDIDATE REGULATIONS

Qualifications
  Governor: 31 years old, state resident for 10 years
  State Senator: 25 years old, district resident for 6 months
  State Representative: 21 years old, district resident for 6 months
Filing Fees
  Governor: $1,500
  State Senate: $200
  State House: $200
Filing Deadlines
  Presidential Primary: December 5
  Independent/Third Party in Presidential Election: July 15
  Congressional Primary: June 9, 2010
  Independent/Third Party in General Election: June 9, 2010 (Independent)
Online Filing: No
Petition Signature Requirements
  Major Party: President: 46,324
  Minor Party: President: 43,913

JUDICIAL ELECTIONS

Justice Chosen: By district
Method of Selection
  Unexpired Term: Gubernatorial appointment from judicial nominating commission
  Full Term: Gubernatorial appointment from judicial nominating commission
No. of Judges: 9

Terms: 6 years
Method of Retention: Retention election

PRIMARY ELECTION PROCESS

Presidential
  Type: Primary/Closed
  Date: February 5, 2008
State
  Type: Primary/Closed
  Date: July 27, 2010

STATE CAMPAIGN FINANCE

Contribution Regulations: No person or family may contribute more than $5,000 to a candidate for state office or to a candidate committee authorized by the candidate to accept contributions or make expenditures on the candidate's behalf during a campaign, and no candidate or candidate committee may knowingly accept a contribution in excess of $5,000 from a person or family during a campaign.
Fundraising Limits: Candidates are not limited to the amount which they are allowed to raise.
Online Filing: No
Reporting Cycle Dates: For state office elections, quarterly reports are due January 31, April 30, July 31, and October 31 (ballot-measure PACs file by 10th of each month).

LOBBYING GUIDELINES

All lobbyists are required to register within 5 days of being employed and pay a $100 registration fee. Yearly reports must then be filed by December 31 detailing lobbyist names, affiliated organizations, or clients and addresses. Twice yearly reports on gifts made must also be filed. Lobbyists are prohibited from making contributions during legislative session.

BALLOT INITIATIVES AND REFERENDUM

Referendum: Yes
Ballot Initiative: Yes
Recall Election: No

OREGON

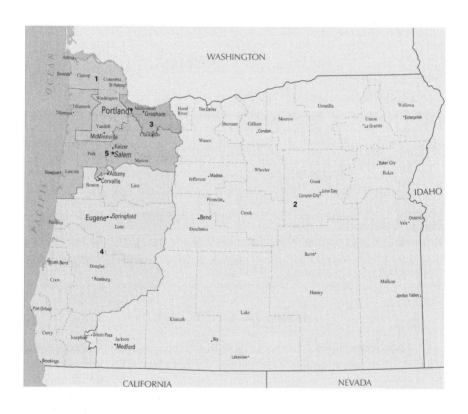

STATE VOTER TURNOUT

Population: 3,747,455
Registered Voters
  2000: 1,943,699
  2002: 1,872,615
  2004: 2,141,249
  2006: 1,976,669
  2008: 2,153,914
Turnout
  2000: 59.1% (Highest Office/Voting-Age Pop.): 1,533,968 / 2,596,823
  2002: 47.2% (Highest Office/Voting-Age Pop.): 1,267,221 / 2,682,501
  2004: 68.8% (Highest Office/Voting-Age Pop.): 1,836,782 / 2,751,312
  2006: 48.4% (Highest Office/Voting-Age Pop.): 1,379,475 / 2,850,525
  2008: 62.3% (Highest Office/Voting-Age Pop.): 1,827,864 / 2,935,131
Youth Turnout (18–29 years old)
  2000: 48%
  2002: 30%
  2004: 55%
  2006: 25%
  2008: 59%

STATEWIDE ELECTION OUTCOMES

Presidential Vote 2004: 1,836,782 votes cast
  Bush (R)   47.2%
  Kerry (D)   51.3%
Presidential Vote 2008: 1,827,864 votes cast
  Obama (D)   56.7%
  McCain (R)   40.4%
Gubernatorial Vote 2006: 1,379,475 votes cast
  Kulongoski (D)   50.7%
  Saxton (R)   42.8%
Electoral College Votes: 7

VOTING REGULATIONS

Residency Requirements: Oregon resident
Absentee Ballot: Yes

Criteria: Available for voters who live out of state or know they will be absent on day of election. Ballots available beginning 45 days prior to election.

Advance Voting: Yes

Criteria: Dates and times for early in person and by mail vary by county.

Provisional Balloting: Yes

Vote by Phone: Yes

Registration Deadline: 21 days prior to election

Secretary of State Website: http://www.sos.state.or.us/elections/

CANDIDATE REGULATIONS

Qualifications
   Governor: 30 years old, state resident for 3 years
   State Senator: 21 years old, district resident for 1 year
   State Representative: 21 years old, district resident for 1 year
Filing Fees
   Governor: $100
   State Senate: $25
   State House: $25
Filing Deadlines
   Presidential Primary: March 11
   Independent/Third Party in Presidential Election: August 26
   Congressional Primary: March 9, 2010
   Independent/Third Party in General Election: August 24, 2010
Online Filing: Yes
Petition Signature Requirements
   Major Party: President: 20,640
   Minor Party: President: 18,356

JUDICIAL ELECTIONS

Justice Chosen: At large

Method of Selection
   Unexpired Term: Gubernatorial appointment
   Full Term: Nonpartisan election

No. of Judges: 7

Terms: 6 years

Method of Retention: Nonpartisan election

PRIMARY ELECTION PROCESS

Presidential
 Type: Primary/Closed
 Date: May 20, 2008
State
 Type: Primary/Closed
 Date: May 18, 2010

STATE CAMPAIGN FINANCE

Contribution Regulations: A tax credit of not more than $50 is allowed for political contributions.
Fundraising Limits: Candidates are not limited to the amount they are allowed to raise.
Online Filing: No
Reporting Cycle Dates: For candidates and committees, reports are due 46–36 days and 15–12 days before election and 21–30 days after election.

LOBBYING GUIDELINES

All lobbyists are required to register within 3 days of being employed. All registrations expire December 31 of odd numbered years. All lobbyists must file quarterly expenditure reports with the Ethics Commission.

BALLOT INITIATIVES AND REFERENDUM

Referendum: Yes
Ballot Initiative: Yes
Recall Election: Yes

PENNSYLVANIA

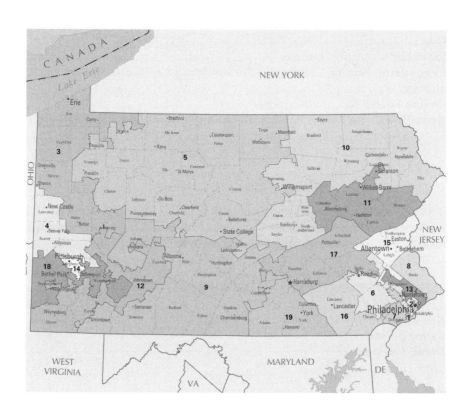

STATE VOTER TURNOUT

Population: 12,432,792
Registered Voters
  2000: 7,781,997
  2002: 7,835,775
  2004: 8,366,455
  2006: 8,812,876
  2008: 8,757,545
Turnout
  2000: 52.3% (Highest Office/Voting-Age Pop.): 4,912,185 / 9,375,373
  2002: 37.3% (Highest Office/Voting-Age Pop.): 3,545,431 / 9,439,137
  2004: 60.6% (Highest Office/Voting-Age Pop.): 5,769,590 / 9,516,922
  2006: 42.6% (Highest Office/Voting-Age Pop.): 4,096,077 / 9,612,380
  2008: 61.8% (Highest Office/Voting-Age Pop.): 5,995,137 / 9,699,676
Youth Turnout (18–29 years old)
  2000: 34%
  2002: 21%
  2004: 48%
  2006: 25%
  2008: 53%

STATEWIDE ELECTION OUTCOMES

Presidential Vote 2004: 5,465,764 votes cast
  Bush (R)   48.5%
  Kerry (D)   51.0%
Presidential Vote 2008: 5,995,137 votes cast
  Obama (D)   54.7%
  McCain (R)   44.3%
Gubernatorial Vote 2006: 4,092,652 votes cast
  Rendell (D)   60.4%
  Swann (R)   39.6%
Electoral College Votes: 21

VOTING REGULATIONS

Residency Requirements: U.S. citizen for 1 month; state and district resident for 30 days
Absentee Ballot: Yes

Criteria: Available for voters who expect to be absent due to electoral duties, occupation, business, illness, disability, or religious beliefs. Must be requested by 5:00 p.m. on Friday prior to election. Must be received by 8:00 p.m. on day of election.

Advance Voting: Yes

Criteria: Available only through absentee ballot process.

Provisional Balloting: Yes

Vote by Phone: No

Registration Deadline: 30 days prior to election.

Secretary of State Website: http://www.dos.state.pa.us/bcel/site/

CANDIDATE REGULATIONS

Qualifications
  Governor: 30 years old, state resident for 7 years
  State Senator: 25 years old, district resident for 1 year, state resident for 4 years, U.S. citizen for 4 years
  State Representative: 21 years old, district resident for 1 year, state resident for 4 years, U.S. citizen for 4 years

Filing Fees
  Governor: $200
  State Senate: $100
  State House: $100

Filing Deadlines
  Presidential Primary: February 12
  Independent/Third Party in Presidential Election: August 1
  Congressional Primary: March 9, 2010, 5:00 p.m.
  Independent/Third Party in General Election: August 2, 2010, 5:00 p.m.

Online Filing No

Petition Signature Requirements
  Major Party: President: No requirement
  Minor Party: President: 24,666

JUDICIAL ELECTIONS

Justice Chosen: At large

Method of Selection
  Unexpired Term: Gubernatorial appointment with consent of the legislature.
  Full Term: Partisan election

No. of Judges: 7

Terms: 10 years
Method of Retention: Retention election

PRIMARY ELECTION PROCESS

Presidential
  Type: Primary/Closed
  Date: April 22, 2008
State
  Type: Primary/Closed
  Date: May 18, 2010

STATE CAMPAIGN FINANCE

Contribution Regulations: Corporations, banks, and associations not founded for political purposes are not allowed to contribute; however, they may establish and administer a separate segregated fund created by voluntary contributions. There are no limitations on the amount of contributions that may be made. Cash contributions are limited to $100.
Fundraising Limits: Candidates are not limited to the amount they are allowed to raise.
Electronic Filing: Yes.
Reporting Cycle Dates: Reports must be filed by the 6th Tuesday and 2nd Friday before the primary and general election as well as 30 days after an election and an annual report on January 31 of each year.

LOBBYING GUIDELINES

All lobbyists are required to register within 10 days of engaging in lobbying activities and file reports annually.

BALLOT INITIATIVES AND REFERENDUM

Referendum: No
Ballot Initiative: No
Recall Election: No

Rhode Island

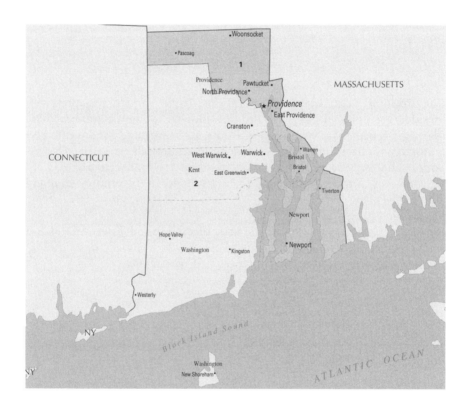

STATE VOTER TURNOUT

Population: 1,057,832
Registered Voters
  2000: 655,107
  2002: 613,037
  2004: 707,234
  2006: 682,344
  2008: 845,805
Turnout
  2000: 50.7% (Highest Office/Voting-Age Pop.): 408,783 / 805,300
  2002: 40.1% (Highest Office/Voting-Age Pop.): 331,834 / 820,755
  2004: 52.9% (Highest Office/Voting-Age Pop.): 437,134 / 826,930
  2006: 46.7% (Highest Office/Voting-Age Pop.): 384,993 / 824,854
  2008: 57.2% (Highest Office/Voting-Age Pop.): 469,767 / 821,425
Youth Turnout (18–29 years old)
  2000: 43%
  2002: 20%
  2004: 44%
  2006: 35%
  2008: 53%

STATEWIDE ELECTION OUTCOMES

Presidential Vote 2004: 437,134 votes cast
  Bush (R)   38.7%
  Kerry (D)   59.4%
Presidential Vote 2008: 469,767 votes cast
  Obama (D)   63.1%
  McCain (R) 35.2%
Gubernatorial Vote 2006: 386,809 votes cast
  Carcieri (R) 51.0%
  Fogarty (D) 49.0%
Electoral College Votes: 4

VOTING REGULATIONS

Residency Requirements: Rhode Island city or town resident
Absentee Ballot: Yes
  Criteria: Available for voters absent from state during all polling hours, or absent due to higher education, illness, disability, religious beliefs,

incarceration, military service, or electoral duties. Must be requested by 4:00 p.m. 21 days prior to election.

Advance Voting: No

Provisional Balloting: Yes

Vote by Phone: No

Registration Deadline: 30 days prior to election except for presidential election, for which voters may register on day of election

Secretary of State Website: http://www.elections.state.ri.us/

CANDIDATE REGULATIONS

Qualifications
  Governor: 18 years old, state resident
  State Senator: 18 years old, state resident
  State Representative: 18 years old, state resident
Filing Fees
  Governor: $0
  State Senate: $0
  State House: $0
Filing Deadlines
  Presidential Primary: December 7
  Independent/Third Party in Presidential Election: September 5, 4:00 p.m.
  Congressional Primary: June 30, 2010
  Independent/Third Party in General Election: June 30, 2010 (Independent)
Online Filing: No
Petition Signature Requirements
  Major Party: President: 1,000
  Minor Party: President: 1,000

JUDICIAL ELECTIONS

Justice Chosen: At large

Method of Selection
  Unexpired Term: Gubernatorial appointment from judicial nominating commission.
  Full Term: Gubernatorial appointment from judicial nominating commission.

No. of Judges: 5

Terms: Life

Method of Retention: Serve during good behavior

PRIMARY ELECTION PROCESS

Presidential
  Type: Primary/Semiclosed
  Date: March 4, 2008
State
  Type: Primary/Semiclosed
  Date: September 14, 2010

STATE CAMPAIGN FINANCE

Contribution Regulations: Only individuals, political action committees, and candidate or officeholder committees may make contributions. The aggregate contributions made by a contributor in a calendar year are limited: (1) by a person or political action committee—$1,000 per recipient (except contributions to a political party for organizational and party-building activities), (2) by a person to all recipients—$10,000, (3) by a non-ballot-question political action committee to all recipients—$25,000, (4) by a person, political action committee, or political party committee to a political party committee for organizational and party-building activities—$10,000, (5) by a political party to any one party candidate—$25,000 (no limit on allowable in-kind contributions), and (6) by a political party committee to all candidates of the party—unlimited. The limit on contributions by a person or political action committee to a candidate for general office increases to $2,000 if the candidate qualifies to receive public funding. Candidate contributions to the candidate's own campaign generally are unlimited; however, for a candidate for general office who has qualified for and elected to receive public funding, contributions (and loans) by the candidate may not exceed 5% of the total the candidate is permitted to spend in the campaign.
Fundraising Limits: Candidates are not limited to the amount they are allowed to raise.
Electronic Filing: Yes.
Reporting Cycle Dates: Preelection reports at 90-day intervals after the 90-day period (April 30, July 20, October 30, and January 30) notwithstanding that the initial report may cover a shorter period (preelection quarterly report). If the 30-day deadline following the initial 90-day reporting period occurs less than 28 days before an election, the 28-day and 7-day preelection reports will be filed. If any 90-day period ends less than 40 days before an elections, the 90-day report is included as part of the report to be filed on the 28th day next preceding day of the election.

In a contested election, on the 28th and 7th days before an election with special provisions for special primary election.

Political party annual report must be filed not later than March 1 each year.

LOBBYING GUIDELINES

All lobbyists are required to register electronically with the Secretary of State. At the time of registration the lobbyist must also file a financial disclosure report that will then be required no later than 30 days after each required reporting period (January 1–June 30 and July 1–December 31).

BALLOT INITIATIVES AND REFERENDUM

Referendum: No
Ballot Initiative: No
Recall Election: Yes

SOUTH CAROLINA

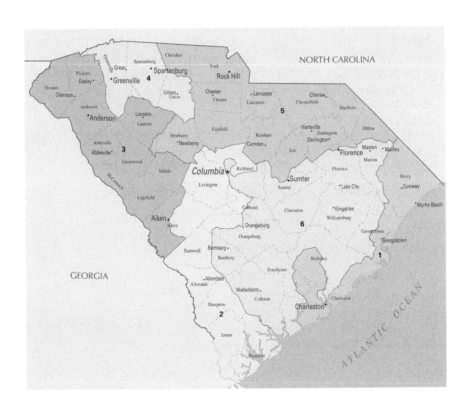

STATE VOTER TURNOUT

Population: 4,407,709
Registered Voters
  2000: 2,157,006
  2002: 2,047,368
  2004: 2,318,235
  2006: 2,452,718
  2008: 2,452,718
Turnout
  2000: 45.7% (Highest Office/Voting-Age Pop.): 1,382,717 / 3,024,476
  2002: 35.6% (Highest Office/Voting-Age Pop.): 1,102,010 / 3,097,576
  2004: 50.7% (Highest Office/Voting-Age Pop.): 1,617,730 / 3,188,222
  2006: 33.1% (Highest Office/Voting-Age Pop.): 1,091,952 / 3,303,593
  2008: 56.5% (Highest Office/Voting-Age Pop.): 1,941,480 / 3,435,500
Youth Turnout (18–29 years old)
  2000: 42%
  2002: 27%
  2004: 46%
  2006: 24%
  2008: 53%

STATEWIDE ELECTION OUTCOMES

Presidential Vote 2004: 1,617,730 votes cast
  Bush (R)   57.8%
  Kerry (D)   40.9%
Presidential Vote 2008: 1,920,969 votes cast
  Obama (D)   53.9%
  McCain (R)   44.9%
Gubernatorial Vote 2006: 1,091,952 votes cast
  Sanford (R)   55.1%
  Moore (D)   44.8%
Electoral College Votes: 8

VOTING REGULATIONS

Residency Requirements: South Carolina resident
Absentee Ballot: Yes
  Criteria: Available for students, voters 65 years of age and older, and
  for voters who are absent from polls due to illness, disability, death in

the family, electoral duties, incarceration, vacation, or employment. May be requested beginning January 1 for any election in that year and ending 4 days prior to election by mail and 5:00 p.m. on day prior to election in person.

Advance Voting: Yes

Criteria: In person absentee voting available beginning as soon as ballots are available and ending 5:00 p.m. on day prior to election.

Provisional Balloting: Yes

Vote by Phone: No

Registration Deadline: 30 days prior to election.

Secretary of State Website: http://www.scvotes.org/

CANDIDATE REGULATIONS

Qualifications

Governor: 30 years old, state resident for 5 years, U.S. citizen for 5 years

State Senator: 25 years old, district resident, state resident

State Representative: 21 years old, district resident, state resident

Filing Fees

Governor: $4,243.12

State Senate: $416

State House: $208

Filing Deadlines

Presidential Primary: November 1, 12:00 p.m.

Independent/Third Party in Presidential Election: July 15, 12:00 p.m. (Independent)

Congressional Primary: March 30, 2010, 12:00 p.m.

Independent/Third Party in General Election: July 15, 2010, 12:00 p.m. (Independent)

Online Filing: No

Petition Signature Requirements

Major Party: President: 10,000

Minor Party: President: 10,000

JUDICIAL ELECTIONS

Justice Chosen: At large

Method of Selection

Unexpired Term: Legislative appointment

Full Term: Legislative appointment

No. of Judges: 5
Terms: 10 years
Method of Retention: Legislative appointment

PRIMARY ELECTION PROCESS

Presidential
 Type: Primary/Open
 Date: Democrats: January 26; Republicans: January 19
State
 Type: Primary/Open
 Date: June 8, 2010

STATE CAMPAIGN FINANCE

Contribution Regulations: Contributions to candidates by other than political parties are limited per each election to $3,500 for any statewide office candidate or $1,000 for any other candidate. A political party may not contribute in the aggregate during an election cycle more than $50,000 for any statewide office candidate or $5,000 for any other candidate. Contributions to a committee are limited to $3,500 in a calendar year.
Fundraising Limits: Candidates are not limited to the amount they are allowed to raise.
Electronic Filing: Yes.
Reporting Cycle Dates: Initial report: If receipt or expenditures of contributions exceeds $500, 10 days after threshold amount met; if $500 threshold not met, 15 days before an election. Subsequent reports: 10 days after each calendar quarter, whether before or after an election, and 15 days before an election; however, if a preelection report is due within 30 days of the end of the quarter, a combined report is due no later than 15 days before the election. Independent expenditure by committee within 20 days before an election to be reported immediately if more than $10,000 for statewide office candidate or $2,000 for any other candidate. Final reports may be filed at any time when contributions no longer received or expenditures made or incurred.

LOBBYING GUIDELINES

All lobbyists must file a report with the State Ethics Commission covering that lobbyist's principal's expenditures attributable to lobbying during that filing period no later than April 10 and October 10 of each year. The filing periods are from January 1 to March 31 for the April 10 report and from April 1 to September 30 for the October 10 report. Any lobbying activity not reflected on the October 10 report and not reported in a termination report must be reported no later December 31 of that year. Each report must be in a form prescribed by the Commission and be limited to and contain, among other information, any contributions made by the lobbyists principle to any candidate or public official, including itemization of (1) the name and address of the public official or candidate to whom the contribution was made, (2) the amount of the contribution, and (3) the date of the contribution.

BALLOT INITIATIVES AND REFERENDUM

Referendum: No
Ballot Initiative: No
Recall Election: No

SOUTH DAKOTA

STATE VOTER TURNOUT

Population: 796,214
Registered Voters
 2000: 471,152
 2002: 471,152
 2004: 502,261
 2006: 503,086
 2008: 530,462
Turnout
 2000: 56.9% (Highest Office/Voting-Age Pop.): 316,269 / 554,933
 2002: 59.7% (Highest Office/Voting-Age Pop.): 337,497 / 565,917
 2004: 66.9% (Highest Office/Voting-Age Pop.): 388,215 / 580,342
 2006: 56.4% (Highest Office/Voting-Age Pop.): 335,508 / 594,599
 2008: 62.8% (Highest Office/Voting-Age Pop.): 381,975 / 608,072
Youth Turnout (18–29 years old)
 2000: 31%
 2002: 36%
 2004: 49%
 2006: 39%
 2008: 44%

STATEWIDE ELECTION OUTCOMES

Presidential Vote 2004: 388,215 votes cast
 Bush (R) 59.9%
 Kerry (D) 38.4%
Presidential Vote 2008: 381,975 votes cast
 Obama (D) 44.7%
 McCain (R) 53.2%
Gubernatorial Vote 2006: 335,508 votes cast
 Rounds (R) 61.7%
 Billion (D) 36.1%
Electoral College Votes: 3

VOTING REGULATIONS

Residency Requirements: South Dakota resident
Absentee Ballot: Yes
 Criteria: Available to all voters. Must be requested by 3:00 p.m. on day
 of election. Must be returned by close of polls on day of election.

Advance Voting: Yes
  Criteria: Available through absentee ballot process: voters may apply for absentee ballot and immediately cast vote in person in county auditor's office prior to day of election.
Provisional Balloting: Yes
Vote by Phone: No
Registration Deadline: 15 days prior to election.
Secretary of State Website: http://www.sdsos.gov/electionsvote registration/electionsvoteregistration_overview.shtm

CANDIDATE REGULATIONS

Qualifications
  Governor: 21 years old, state resident for 2 years
  State Senator: 21 years old, state resident for 2 years
  State Representative: 21 years old, state resident for 2 years
Filing Fees
  Governor: $0
  State Senate: $0
  State House: $0
Filing Deadlines
  Presidential Primary: March 25
  Independent/Third Party in Presidential Election: August 5
  Congressional Primary: March 30, 2010
  Independent/Third Party in General Election: June 8, 2010 (Independent)
Online Filing: No
Petition Signature Requirements
  Major Party: President: 8,389
  Minor Party: President: 3,356

JUDICIAL ELECTIONS

Justice Chosen: Initially chosen by district; retention chosen statewide.
Method of Selection
  Unexpired Term: Gubernatorial appointment from judicial nominating commission.
  Full Term: Gubernatorial appointment from judicial nominating commission.
No. of Judges: 5
Terms: 8 years
Method of Retention: Retention election

PRIMARY ELECTION PROCESS

Presidential
  Type: Primary/Closed
  Date: June 3, 2008
State
  Type: Primary/Closed
  Date: June 8, 2010

STATE CAMPAIGN FINANCE

Contribution Regulations: No individual may contribute in a calendar year more than $1,000 to or on behalf of a state office candidate or more than $250 to or on behalf of a legislative or county office candidate; however, there is no limit for the candidate, the candidate's spouse, and certain relatives of the candidate and their spouses. Contributions to a political party by an individual are limited to $3,000 in a calendar year. Candidates and candidates' committees, political action committees, and political party committees may receive contributions only from individuals, political action committees, and political party committees. Corporations may not make contributions except to a ballot question committee, and associations may make contributions but not out of dues or treasury funds.

Fundraising Limits: Candidates are not limited to the amount they are allowed to raise.

Electronic Filing: No.

Reporting Cycle Dates: State office candidates, candidates' committees, political action committees, and political party committees: Last Tuesday prior to primary and general election, and by February 1 for preceding calendar year or remainder not covered by previous report. Legislative and county office candidates: By July 1 and December 31 of election year.

LOBBYING GUIDELINES

Lobbyists must register with the Secretary of State and pay a registration fee of $35 unless the lobbyist is lobbying for him- or herself. All lobbyists and lobbyist employers must complete expense reports that are due in the Office of the Secretary of State July 1 of each year.

BALLOT INITIATIVES AND REFERENDUM

Referendum: Yes
Ballot Initiative: Yes
Recall Election: No

TENNESSEE

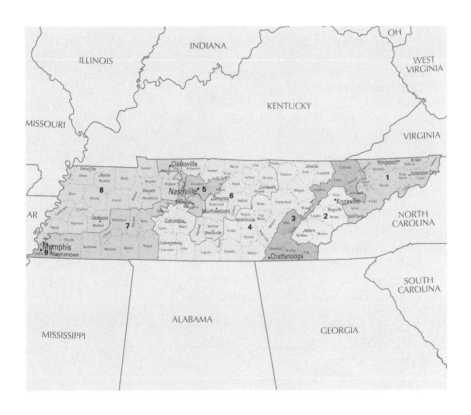

STATE VOTER TURNOUT

Population: 6,214,888
Registered Voters
  2000: 3,181,108
  2002: 3,134,104
  2004: 3,748,235
  2006: 3,738,703
  2008: 3,994,554
Turnout
  2000: 48.1% (Highest Office/Voting-Age Pop.): 2,076,181 / 4,318,729
  2002: 37.3% (Highest Office/Voting-Age Pop.): 1,644,741 / 4,403,334
  2004: 54.1% (Highest Office/Voting-Age Pop.): 2,437,319 / 4,504,297
  2006: 39.5% (Highest Office/Voting-Age Pop.): 1,833,695 / 4,636,679
  2008: 54.7% (Highest Office/Voting-Age Pop.): 2,599,749 / 4,753,314
Youth Turnout (18-29 years old)
  2000: 30%
  2002: 21%
  2004: 40%
  2006: 23%
  2008: 46%

STATEWIDE ELECTION OUTCOMES

Presidential Vote 2004: 2,437,319 votes cast
  Bush (R)   56.8%
  Kerry (D)   42.5%
Presidential Vote 2008: 2,599,749 votes cast
  Obama (D)   41.8%
  McCain (R)   56.9%
Gubernatorial Vote 2006: 1,818,549 votes cast
  Bredesen (D) 68.6%
  Bryson (R)   29.7%
Electoral College Votes: 11

VOTING REGULATIONS

Residency Requirements: Tennessee resident
Absentee Ballot: Yes
  Criteria: Available for voters who are absent from county throughout
  early voting period and day of election; medically unable to reach polls,

as attested by a licensed physician; 65 or older; ill or disabled; engaged in electoral duties; observing a religious holiday; studying at an accredited institution outside of county; working outside county under a commercial driver's license; or are incarcerated. May be requested beginning 90 days prior to election and ending 7 days prior to election. Must be returned by close of polls on day of election.

Advance Voting: Yes

Criteria: Available for all voters; no excuse is necessary. Generally begins 20 days prior to election and ends 5 days prior to election. In city election with no opposition on ballot, early voting begins 10 days prior to election.

Provisional Balloting: Yes

Vote by Phone: No

Registration Deadline: 30 days prior to election.

Secretary of State Website: http://tn.gov/sos/election/

CANDIDATE REGULATIONS

Qualifications

Governor: 30 years old, state resident for 7 years

State Senator: 30 years old, district resident for 1 year, state resident for 3 years

State Representative: 21 years old, district resident for 1 year, state resident for 3 years

Filing Fees

Governor: $0

State Senate: $0

State House: $0

Filing Deadlines

Presidential Primary: December 4

Independent/Third Party in Presidential Election: August 21, 12:00 p.m. (Independent)

Congressional Primary: April 1, 2010

Independent/Third Party in General Election: April 1, 2010 (Indepedent)

Online Filing: No

Petition Signature Requirements:

Major Party: President: 2,500

Minor Party: President: 275

JUDICIAL ELECTIONS

Justice Chosen: At large
Method of Selection
  Unexpired Term: Gubernatorial appointment from judicial nominating commission.
  Full Term: Gubernatorial appointment from judicial nominating commission.
No. of Judges: 5
Terms: 8 years
Method of Retention: Retention election

PRIMARY ELECTION PROCESS

Presidential
  Type: Primary/Open
  Date: February 5, 2008
State
  Type: Primary/Open
  Date: August 5, 2010

STATE CAMPAIGN FINANCE

Contribution Regulations: Persons, excluding candidates and multi-candidate political committees, may not make a contribution larger than $2,500 for a statewide office election and $1,000 for a candidate for other office. Multicandidate political campaign committees may contribute no more than $7,500 to a statewide candidate and $5,000 to a candidate for other office. Candidates may make contributions using personal funds as long as it does not exceed $250,000 for a statewide office, $40,000 for a state senate, and $20,000 for other office. All contributions made by all political campaign committees controlled by a political party or party caucus may not exceed $250,000 per election for a statewide candidate, $40,000 for a state senate candidate, and $20,00 for other office.
Fundraising Limits: Candidates are not limited to the amount they are allowed to raise.
Electronic Filing: No.
Reporting Cycle Dates: Reports must be filed by February 1 each year through year of election; in election year, 7 days before and 48 days after each election if political treasure appointed more than 1 year before election. Multicandidate political campaign committees: within 10 days after each quarter.

LOBBYING GUIDELINES

All lobbyists are required to file a sworn report annually. The report is from June 30 or through the day following the end of the regular annual session of the general assembly, whichever is later, and must be filed with the Registry of Election Finance not later than 30 days after the period covered.

BALLOT INITIATIVES AND REFERENDUM

Referendum: No
Ballot Initiative: No
Recall Election: No

Texas

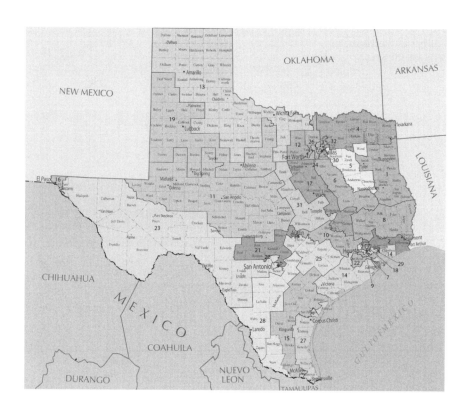

STATE VOTER TURNOUT

Population: 23,904,380
Registered Voters
  2000: 10,267,639
  2002: 10,334,773
  2004: 13,098,329
  2006: 13,074,279
  2008: 13,575,062
Turnout
  2000: 42.4% (Highest Office/Voting-Age Pop.): 6,407,037 / 15,148,121
  2002: 28.8% (Highest Office/Voting-Age Pop.): 4,514,012 / 15,747,290
  2004: 45.4% (Highest Office/Voting-Age Pop.): 7,410,765 / 16,317,281
  2006: 25.8% (Highest Office/Voting-Age Pop.): 4,399,068 / 17,038,979
  2008: 45.5% (Highest Office/Voting-Age Pop.): 8,077,795 / 17,735,442
Youth Turnout (18–29 years old)
  2000: 35%
  2002: 17%
  2004: 42%
  2006: 17%
  2008: 39%

STATEWIDE ELECTION OUTCOMES

Presidential Vote 2004: 7,410,765 votes cast
  Bush (R)   61.1%
  Kerry (D)   38.2%
Presidential Vote 2008: 8,077,795 votes cast
  Obama (D)   43.7%
  McCain (R)   55.5%
Gubernatorial Vote 2006: 4,399,116 votes cast
  Perry (R)   39.0%
  Bell (D)   29.8%
Electoral College Votes: 34

VOTING REGULATIONS

Residency Requirements: County resident
Absentee Ballot: Yes
  Criteria: Available for voters absent from county during early-voting
  period and day of election, and for those 65 and older, incarcerated,

ill, or disabled. May be requested beginning 60 days prior to election and ending 7 days prior to election, or on the last business day before the 7th day before election if it falls on a weekend or holiday.

Advance Voting: Yes

Criteria: Available to all voters beginning 17 days prior to election, or 12 days prior to May election, and ending 4 days prior to election.

Provisional Balloting: Yes

Vote by Phone: No

Registration Deadline: 30 days prior to election.

Secretary of State Website: http://www.sos.state.tx.us/elections/index.shtml

CANDIDATE REGULATIONS

Qualifications

Governor: 30 years old, state resident for 5 years

State Senator: 26 years old, district resident for 1 year, state resident for 5 years

State Representative: 21 years old, district resident for 1 year, state resident for 2 years

Filing Fees

Governor: $3,750

State Senate: $1,250 (for partisan candidates)

State House: $750 (for partisan candidates)

Filing Deadlines

Presidential Primary: January 2

Independent/Third Party in Presidential Election: May 8 (Independent)

Congressional Primary: January 4, 2010, 6:00 p.m.

Independent/Third Party in General Election: May 13, 2010 (Independent); May 23, 2010 (Third Party)

Online Filing: No

Petition Signature Requirements

Major Party: President: 43,991

Minor Party: President: 74,108 (Voters who did not vote in either presidential primary)

JUDICIAL ELECTIONS

Justice Chosen: At large
Method of Selection
  Unexpired Term: Gubernatorial appointment
  Full Term: Partisan election
No. of Judges: 9
Terms: 6 years
Method of Retention: Partisan election

PRIMARY ELECTION PROCESS

Presidential
  Type: Primary/Open
  Date: March 4, 2008
State
  Type: Primary/Open
  Date: March 2, 2010

STATE CAMPAIGN FINANCE

Contribution Regulations: There are no limits to the contributions that can be made except in judicial elections.
Fundraising Limits: Candidates may not knowingly make or authorize a campaign expenditure or accept a campaign contribution totaling more than $500 or accept political contributions more than $500 at a time when a campaign treasurer appointment for the candidate committee is not in effect.
Electronic Filing: No.
Reporting Cycle Dates: Semiannual reports are due by July 15 and January 31.

LOBBYING GUIDELINES

The yearly lobby registration fee is $500 for all registrants except organizations exempt from federal taxes under the IRS Code, 26 U.S.C. §

501(c)(3) or 501(c)(4) and lobbyists who represent only such organizations. The yearly fee for those registrants is $100. Registration must be made within 5 days of being hired and registrations expire on December 31. Lobby activity reports for monthly filers are due by the 10th day of each month and cover activities occurring during the preceding calendar month. Annual filers submit 1 report for the entire calendar year by January 10 of the following year.

BALLOT INITIATIVES AND REFERENDUM

Referendum: No
Ballot Initiative: No
Recall Election: No

UTAH

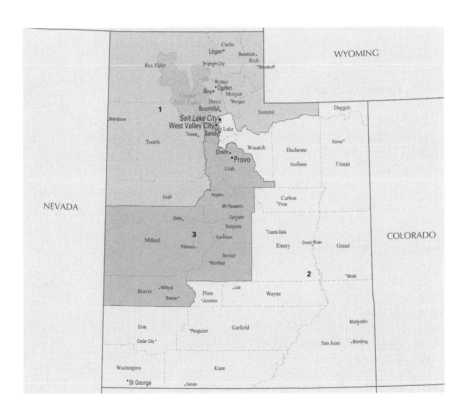

STATE VOTER TURNOUT

Population: 2,645,330
Registered Voters
  2000: 1,123,238
  2002: 1,118,175
  2004: 1,278,912
  2006: 1,302,405
  2008: 1,432,525
Turnout
  2000: 50.3% (Highest Office/Voting-Age Pop.): 770,754 / 1,536,804
  2002: 35.0% (Highest Office/Voting-Age Pop.): 557,153 / 1,612,887
  2004: 54.7% (Highest Office/Voting-Age Pop.): 927,844 / 1,694,751
  2006: 31.8% (Highest Office/Voting-Age Pop.): 571,252 / 1,797,941
  2008: 50.9% (Highest Office/Voting-Age Pop.): 971,185 / 1,906,216
Youth Turnout (18–29 years old)
  2000: 40%
  2002: 22%
  2004: 56%
  2006: 17%
  2008: 37%

STATEWIDE ELECTION OUTCOMES

Presidential Vote 2004: 942,010 votes cast
  Bush (R)   71.5%
  Kerry (D)   26.0%
Presidential Vote 2008: 952,370 votes cast
  Obama (D)   34.4%
  McCain (R)   62.6%
Gubernatorial Vote 2008: 945,525 votes cast
  Huntsman (R)   77.6%
  Springmeyer (D)   19.7%
Electoral College Votes: 5

VOTING REGULATIONS

Residency Requirements: Utah resident for 30 days
Absentee Ballot: Yes
  Criteria: Available for all voters. Must be requested by Friday prior to election. Must be received before 12:00 p.m. on day of election and postmarked prior to day of election.

Advance Voting: Yes
    Criteria: Available for all voters; no excuse is necessary. Dates and times vary by county. Early voting ends at close of business on day prior to election.
Provisional Balloting: Yes
Vote by Phone: No
Registration Deadline: 30 day prior to election, or in person between 8:00 a.m. and 8:00 p.m. on 15th day prior to election.
Secretary of State Website: http://elections.utah.gov/

CANDIDATE REGULATIONS

Qualifications
    Governor: 30 years old, state resident for 5 years
    State Senator: 25 years old, district resident for 6 months, state resident for 3 years
    State Representative: 25 years old, district resident for 6 month, state resident for 5 years
Filing Fees
    Governor: $536
    State Senate: $32.40
    State House: $16.20
Filing Deadlines
    Presidential Primary: October 15
    Independent/Third Party in Presidential Election: March 17
    Congressional Primary: March 19, 2010, 5:00 p.m.
    Independent/Third Party in General Election: March 19, 2010, 5:00 p.m.
Online Filing: No
Petition Signature Requirements
    Major Party: President: 2,000
    Minor Party: President: 1,000

JUDICIAL ELECTIONS

Justice Chosen: At large
Method of Selection
    Unexpired Term: Gubernatorial appointment from judicial nominating commission with consent of the legislature.
    Full Term: Gubernatorial appointment from judicial nominating commission with consent of the legislature.

No. of Judges: 5
Terms: 10 (Initial term appointment is until next general election following the 3rd years from that appointment.)
Method of Retention: Retention election

PRIMARY ELECTION PROCESS

Presidential
   Type: Primary/Semiclosed
   Date: February 5, 2008
State
   Type: Primary/Semiclosed
   Date: June 22, 2010

STATE CAMPAIGN FINANCE

Contribution Regulations: State executive office, legislative office, and state and local school board office candidate and officeholder, a party committee of a registered political party, a political action committee that receives contributions or makes expenditures of $750 or more in a calendar year, a political issues committee that receives political issues contributions of $750 or more or makes political issue expenditures of $50 or more in a calendar year, a corporation that makes expenditures for political purposes or political issues expenditures of $750 or more in a calendar year, and a judge standing for a retention election to file periodic statements of receipts and expenditures.
Fundraising Limits: Candidates are not limited to the amount they are allowed to raise.
Electronic Filing: Yes
Reporting Cycle Dates: Reports are due 7 days before primary, September 15, and 7 days before general election.

LOBBYING GUIDELINES

Lobbyists must register with the Lieutenant Governor's office and pay a $25 fee. Registrations expire on December 31 of even numbered years. Financial disclosure reports must be filed 4 times each year: January 10, April 10, July 10, and October 10.

BALLOT INITIATIVES AND REFERENDUM

Referendum: Yes
Ballot Initiative: Yes
Recall Election: No

VERMONT

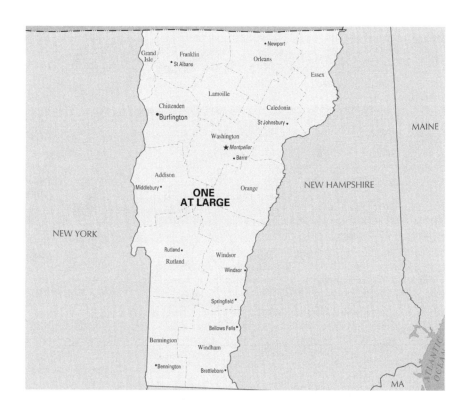

STATE VOTER TURNOUT

Population: 621,254
Registered Voters
  2000: 427,354
  2002: 418,718
  2004: 444,508
  2006: 433,569
  2008: 454,466
Turnout
  2000: 63.1% (Highest Office/Voting-Age Pop.): 294,308 / 463,878
  2002: 48.1% (Highest Office/Voting-Age Pop.): 230,161 / 473,094
  2004: 65.0% (Highest Office/Voting-Age Pop.): 312,309 / 480,803
  2006: 53.8% (Highest Office/Voting-Age Pop.): 262,726 / 487,900
  2008: 66.4% (Highest Office/Voting-Age Pop.): 327,301 / 493,153
Youth Turnout (18–29 years old)
  2000: 40%
  2002: 20%
  2004: 39%
  2006: 26%
  2008: 48%

STATEWIDE ELECTION OUTCOMES

Presidential Vote 2004: 312,309 votes cast
  Bush (R)   38.8%
  Kerry (D)   58.9%
Presidential Vote 2008: 325,046 votes cast
  Obama (D)   67.4%
  McCain (R)   30.4%
Gubernatorial Vote 2008: 319,085 votes cast
  Douglas (R)   53.4%
  Symington (D)   21.7%
Electoral College Votes: 3

VOTING REGULATIONS

Residency Requirements: Vermont resident
Absentee Ballot: Yes
  Criteria: Home-delivered ballots for ill or disabled voters must be requested 3 days prior to election. For other absentee voters, mailed

ballots must be requested by 5:00 p.m. or close of business on day prior to election. Must be returned to polling place by 7:00 p.m. on day of election.

Advance Voting: Yes

Criteria: Available for all voters; no excuse is necessary. Begins 30 days prior to primary or general election and 20 days prior to municipal election.

Provisional Balloting: Yes

Vote by Phone: Yes

Registration Deadline: 5:00 p.m. on Wednesday prior to election.

Secretary of State Website: http://vermont-elections.org/soshome.htm

CANDIDATE REGULATIONS

Qualifications

Governor: 18 years old, state resident for 4 years

State Senator: 18 years old, district resident for 1 year, state resident for 2 years

State Representative: 18 years old, district resident for 1 year, state resident for 2 years

Filing Fees

Governor: $0

State Senate: $0

State House: $0

Filing Deadlines

Presidential Primary: January 21

Independent/Third Party in Presidential Election: September 12

Congressional Primary: July 19, 2010, 5:00 p.m.

Independent/Third Party in General Election: September 17, 2010

Online Filing: No

Petition Signature Requirements

Major Party: President: No requirement

Minor Party: President: 1,000

JUDICIAL ELECTIONS

Justice Chosen: At large

Method of Selection

Unexpired Term: Gubernatorial appointment from judicial nominating commission.

Full Term: Gubernatorial appointment from judicial nominating commission.

No. of Judges: 5
Terms: 6 years
Method of Retention: Legislative appointment

PRIMARY ELECTION PROCESS

Presidential
    Type: Primary/Open
    Date: March 4, 2008
State
    Type: Primary/Open
    Date: September 14, 2010

STATE CAMPAIGN FINANCE

Contribution Regulations: Total contributions that may be accepted from a single source or political committee in any 2-year general-election cycle are limited: (1) candidate for Governor, Lieutenant Governor, Secretary of State, State Treasurer, Auditor of Accounts, or Attorney General—$400; (2) candidate for State Senator or county office—$300; (3) candidates for State Representative or local office—$200; and (4) political committee (other than a political committee of a candidate) or political party—$2,000. Total contributions that may be accepted from a political party in any 2-year general-election cycle are not as restricted: (1) any candidate—no limit, and (2) political committee (other than a political committee of a candidate) or political party—$2,000.

Fundraising Limits: Candidates for the following offices may not exceed the limits indicated in any 2-year general-election cycle:

1. Governor—nonincumbent: $300,000; incumbent: $225,000 (85%).
2. Lieutenant governor—nonincumbent: $100,000; incumbent: $85,000 (85%).
3. Secretary of State, State Treasurer, Auditor of Accounts, or Attorney General—nonincumbent: $45,000; incumbent: $38,250 (85%).
4. State Senator—nonincumbent: $4,000 plus an additional $2,500 for each additional seat in the senate district; incumbent: $3,600, plus an additional $2,250 for each additional seat in the senate district (90%)

5. State Representatives in a single member district—nonincumbent: $2,000; incumbent: $1,800 (90%).
6. State Representative in a two-member district—nonincumbent: $3,000; incumbent: $2,700 (90%).
7. County Office—nonincumbent: $4,000; incumbent: $4,000 (100%).

Electronic Filing: No.

Reporting Cycle Dates: Reports are due 40 days before primary; 25th day of each month after primary and continuing to general election; not later than 40 days after general election and July 15th in odd-numbered years.

LOBBYING GUIDELINES

Each lobbying firm is required to file a form listing all lobbyists who are employed by, subcontracted by, members of, or affiliated with the firm. This form must be submitted within 48 hours of lobbying activities commencing, and an updated listing must be filed within 48 hours of any changes. Lobbyists who are NOT employed by, subcontracted by, or affiliated with a lobbying firm must disclose compensation paid to the lobbyist and all unreimbursed expenditures made by the lobbyist. Each lobbyist must pay an initial registration fee of $25, plus an additional $5 for each lobbyist employer listed.

BALLOT INITIATIVES AND REFERENDUM

Referendum: No
Ballot Initiative: No
Recall Election: No

VIRGINIA

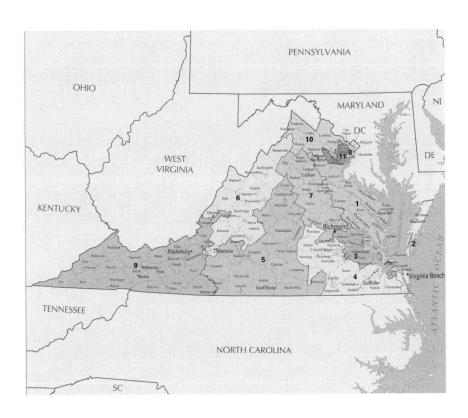

STATE VOTER TURNOUT

Population: 7,712,091
Registered Voters
  2000: 3,770,273
  2002: 3,840,484
  2004: 4,515,675
  2006: 4,555,940
  2008: 4,912,634
Turnout
  2000: 50.9% (Highest Office/Voting-Age Pop.): 2,739,447 / 5,388,039
  2002: 26.9% (Highest Office/Voting-Age Pop.): 1,489,422 / 5,536,473
  2004: 56.2% (Highest Office/Voting-Age Pop.): 3,198,367 / 5,689,368
  2006: 40.6% (Highest Office/Voting-Age Pop.): 2,370,445 / 5,841,335
  2008: 62.9% (Highest Office/Voting-Age Pop.): 3,752,858 / 5,965,880
Youth Turnout (18–29 years old)
  2000: 47%
  2002: 18%
  2004: 43%
  2006: 32%
  2008: 59%

STATEWIDE ELECTION OUTCOMES

Presidential Vote 2004: 3,198,367 votes cast
  Bush (R)   53.7%
  Kerry (D)   45.5%
Presidential Vote 2008: 3,723,260 votes cast
  Obama (D)   52.6%
  McCain (R)   46.3%
Gubernatorial Vote 2005: 1,983,778 votes cast
  Kaine (D)   51.7%
  Kilgore (R)   46.0%
Electoral College Votes: 13

VOTING REGULATIONS

Residency Requirements: Virginia resident
Absentee Ballot: Yes

Criteria: Available for voters absent from polls due to employment, studies, incarceration, electoral duties, illness, or disability, and those 65 or older. Must be requested by Tuesday prior to election.
Advance Voting: Yes
   Criteria: Available as in person absentee (an excuse is necessary) beginning 45 days prior to election and ending 3 days prior to election.
Provisional Balloting: Yes
Vote by Phone: No
Registration Deadline: 29 days prior to election; 13 days prior to special election; 7 days prior to election called by Governor.
Secretary of State Website: http://www.sbe.virginia.gov/cms/

CANDIDATE REGULATIONS

Qualifications
   Governor: 30 years old, state resident for 5 years
   State Senator: 21 years old, district resident, state resident for 1 year
   State Representative: 21 years old, district resident, state resident for 1 year
Filing Fees
   Governor: $3,500 (for primary candidates only)
   State Senate: $360 (for primary candidates only)
   State House: $352.80 (for primary candidates only)
Filing Deadlines
   Presidential Primary: December 14, 5:00 p.m.
   Independent/Third Party in Presidential Election: August 22, 12:00 p.m.
   Congressional Primary: June 9, 2010
   Independent/Third Party in General Election: June 8, 2010 (Independent); June 14, 2010 (Third Party)
Online Filing: No
Petition Signature Requirements
   Major Party: President: No requirement
   Minor Party: President: 10,000

JUDICIAL ELECTIONS

Justice Chosen: At large
Method of Selection
   Unexpired Term: Gubernatorial appointment for interim appointments.

Full Term: Legislative appointment
No. of Judges: 7
Terms: 12 years
Method of Retention: Legislative appointment

PRIMARY ELECTION PROCESS

Presidential
    Type: Primary/Open
    Date: February 12, 2008
State
    Type: Primary/Open
    Date: June 8, 2010

STATE CAMPAIGN FINANCE

Contribution Regulations: Contributions are not limited.
Fundraising Limits: Candidates are not limited to the amount they are allowed to raise.
Electronic Filing: No.
Reporting Cycle Dates: Reports for a nonelection year—July 15 of election year and January 15 of following year. For election year—April, 8th day before June primary, July 15, September 15, October 15, 8th day before November election, 30th day after November election, January 15th of following year.

LOBBYING GUIDELINES

All lobbyists are required to register with the Secretary of the Commonwealth and pay a registration fee of $50. Registrations are required annually and expire April 30. Lobbyist disclosure forms must be filed by July 1 for the 12-month period beginning May 1 and ending April 30.

BALLOT INITIATIVES AND REFERENDUM

Referendum: No
Ballot Initiative: No
Recall Election: No

WASHINGTON

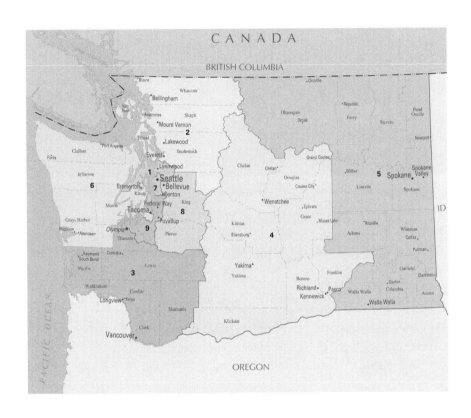

STATE VOTER TURNOUT

Population: 6,468,424
Registered Voters
  2000: 3,335,714
  2002: 3,209,648
  2004: 3,508,208
  2006: 3,264,511
  2008: 3,630,118
Turnout
  2000: 56.2% (Highest Office/Voting-Age Pop.): 2,487,433 / 4,422,086
  2002: 37.9% (Highest Office/Voting-Age Pop.): 1,739,116 / 4,566,977
  2004: 60.8% (Highest Office/Voting-Age Pop.): 2,859,084 / 4,702,007
  2006: 42.7% (Highest Office/Voting-Age Pop.): 2,083,734 / 4,876,661
  2008: 61.0% (Highest Office/Voting-Age Pop.): 3,071,587 / 5,033,380
Youth Turnout (18–29 years old)
  2000: 42%
  2002: 20%
  2004: 53%
  2006: 30%
  2008: 55%

STATEWIDE ELECTION OUTCOMES

Presidential Vote 2004: 2,859,084 votes cast
  Bush (R)   45.6%
  Kerry (D)   52.8%
Presidential Vote 2008: 3,036,878 votes cast
  Obama (D)   57.7%
  McCain (R) 40.5%
Gubernatorial Vote 2008: 3,002,862 votes cast
  Gregoire (D) 53.2%
  Rossi (R)   46.8%
Electoral College Votes: 11

VOTING REGULATIONS

Residency Requirements: State, county, and precinct resident for 30 days.
Absentee Ballot: Yes

Criteria: Available for all voters. Ballots are available at least 20 days prior to election. Must be returned by 8:00 p.m. on day of election.
Advance Voting: No
Provisional Balloting: Yes
Vote by Phone: No
Registration Deadline: 15 days prior to election in person; 30 days prior to election by mail.
Secretary of State Website: http://www.secstate.wa.gov/elections/

CANDIDATE REGULATIONS

Qualifications
  Governor: 18 years old, state resident (qualified elector in state)
  State Senator: 18 years old, district resident (qualified elector)
  State Representative: 18 years old, district resident (qualified elector)
Filing Fees
  Governor: $1,636.18
  State Senate: $412.80
  State House: $412.80
Filing Deadlines
  Presidential Primary: December 21
  Independent/Third Party in Presidential Election: August 2
  Congressional Primary: June 11, 2010
  Independent/Third Party in General Election: June 11, 2010
Online Filing: Yes
Petition Signature Requirements
  Major Party: President: No requirement
  Minor Party: President: 1,000

JUDICIAL ELECTIONS

Justice Chosen: At large
Method of Selection
  Unexpired Term: Gubernatorial appointment
  Full Term: Nonpartisan election
No. of Judges: 9
Terms: 6 years
Method of Retention: Nonpartisan election

PRIMARY ELECTION PROCESS

Presidential
  Type: Caucus/Closed
  Date: February 9, 2008
State
  Type: Caucus/Closed
  Date: August 17, 2010

STATE CAMPAIGN FINANCE

Contribution Regulations: Contributions by each contributor to a candidate for state executive or legislative office by other than the candidate are limited: (1) nonparty and non-legislative-caucus contributions per each election to a state legislative office candidate—$625 and to a state executive office candidate—$1,250, (2) contributions by a political party state organization or caucus political committee per election cycle—64 cents per registered voter in the jurisdiction, and (3) contributions by a major political party county central committee or legislative district committee per election cycle—32 cents per register voter in the jurisdiction. Combined contributions by major party–county central committees and legislative district committee to a state office candidate per election cycle may not exceed 32 cents per registered voter in the jurisdiction. Contributions per calendar year to political parties and caucus political committees by other than individuals, parties, and caucuses are also limited: $625 to a caucus and $3,200 to a party state organization or to a major party–county central committee or legislative district committee. Contributions made by a single contributor other and a major political party state organization within 21 days of the general election may not exceed $50,000 for a statewide office campaign or $5,000 for any other campaign.
Fundraising Limits: Candidates are not limited to the amount they are allowed to raise.
Electronic Filing: Yes.
Reporting Cycle Dates: At time campaign is designated; 21st and 7th day before and by the 10th day of each month in which no other reports are required if contributions received or expenditures made total $200 since last report and at time campaign fund is closed and campaign concluded.

LOBBYING GUIDELINES

Lobbyists must register before doing any lobbying or within 30 days of being employed to lobby, whichever occurs first. Lobbyists must file monthly disclosure reports. Employers of lobbyists must file yearly lobbying expense reports by the last day of February for the previous year.

BALLOT INITIATIVES AND REFERENDUM

Referendum: Yes
Ballot Initiative: Yes
Recall Election: Yes

WEST VIRGINIA

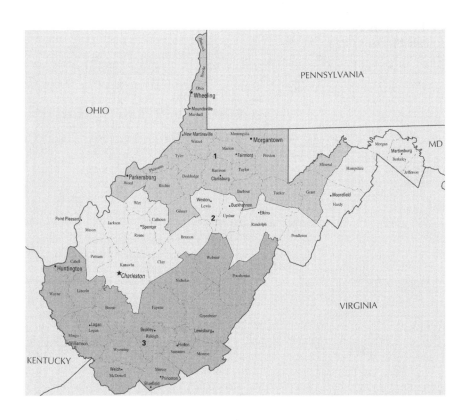

STATE VOTER TURNOUT

Population: 1,812,035
Registered Voters
  2000: 1,067,822
  2002: 1,060,892
  2004: 1,168,694
  2006: 1,137,371
  2008: 1,212,117
Turnout
  2000: 46.1% (Highest Office/Voting-Age Pop.): 648,124 / 1,405,332
  2002: 30.8% (Highest Office/Voting-Age Pop.): 436,183 / 1,408,816
  2004: 53.4% (Highest Office/Voting-Age Pop.): 755,887 / 1,414,991
  2006: 32.3% (Highest Office/Voting-Age Pop.): 459,884 / 1,421,717
  2008: 51.5% (Highest Office/Voting-Age Pop.): 736,799 / 1,429,529
Youth Turnout (18–29 years old)
  2000: 38%
  2002: 15%
  2004: 49%
  2006: 16%
  2008: 48%

STATEWIDE ELECTION OUTCOMES

Presidential Vote 2004: 755,887 votes cast
  Bush (R)   56.1%
  Kerry (D)   43.2%
Presidential Vote 2008: 713,439 votes cast
  Obama (D)   42.6%
  McCain (R)   55.7%
Gubernatorial Vote 2008: 760,047 votes cast
  Manchin (D) 60.9%
  Weeks (R)   25.7%
Electoral College Votes: 5

VOTING REGULATIONS

Residency Requirements: State and county resident
Absentee Ballot: Yes
  Criteria: Available for all voters. May be requested starting 8 weeks prior to election and ending 6 days prior to election.

Advance Voting: Yes
   Criteria: Begins 20 days prior to election and ends 3 days prior to election. Available during regular business hours and possibly on two Saturdays prior to election.
Provisional Balloting: Yes
Vote by Phone: No
Registration Deadline: 21 days prior to election.
Secretary of State Website: http://www.wvsos.com/elections/main.htm

CANDIDATE REGULATIONS

Qualifications
   Governor: 30 years old, state resident for 5 years
   State Senator: 25 years old, district resident for 1 year, state resident for 5 years
   State Representative: 18 years old, district resident for 1 year, state resident
Filing Fees
   Governor: $1,500
   State Senate: $150
   State House: $75
Filing Deadlines
   Presidential Primary: January 26
   Independent/Third Party in Presidential Election: August 1
   Congressional Primary: January 30, 2010
   Independent/Third Party in General Election: July 30, 2010
Online Filing: No
Petition Signature Requirements
   Major Party: President: No requirement
   Minor Party: President: 15,118 (2% of voters during last presidential election)

JUDICIAL ELECTIONS

Justice Chosen: At large
Method of Selection
   Unexpired Term: Generational appointment (only good until next election year)
   Full Term: Partisan election
No. of Judges: 5

Terms: 12 years
Method of Retention: Partisan election

PRIMARY ELECTION PROCESS

Presidential
  Type: Democrats: Primary/Semiclosed; Republicans: Caucus/Closed
  Date: May 13, 2008
State
  Type: Democrats: Primary/Semiclosed; Republicans: Caucus/Closed
  Date: May 11, 2010

STATE CAMPAIGN FINANCE

Contribution Regulations: Contributions by any person, including a political action committee, to a maximum of $1,000 to or on behalf of a candidate in a primary or general election campaign and a maximum of $1,000 to a political party state executive committee in a calendar year. Corporations are not permitted to make candidate-related contributions but may establish a political action committee.
Fundraising Limits: Candidates are not limited to the amount they are allowed to raise.
Electronic Filing: No
Reporting Cycle Dates: Reports are due the last Saturday in March or within 15 days thereafter before the primary; 7–10 days before and 25–30 days after a primary, general, or special election.

LOBBYING GUIDELINES

All lobbyists must complete a lobbyist training session each legislative session. Lobbyists must register with the House before lobbying and pay a registration fee of $100 per lobbyist, plus $100 for each additional entity represented. Registrations expire at the end of each even numbered year.

BALLOT INITIATIVES AND REFERENDUM

Referendum: No
Ballot Initiative: No
Recall Election: No

WISCONSIN

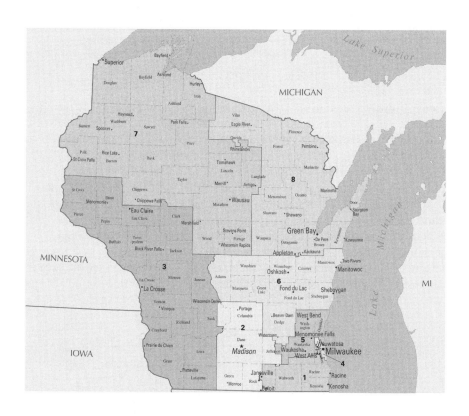

STATE VOTER TURNOUT

Population: 5,601,640
Registered Voters
  2000: n/a
  2002: n/a
  2004: n/a
  2006: n/a
  2008: 3,688,195
Turnout
  2000: 64.5% (Highest Office/Voting-Age Pop.): 2,598,607 / 4,018,183
  2002: 43.2% (Highest Office/Voting-Age Pop.): 1,775,349 / 4,100,477
  2004: 71.6% (Highest Office/Voting-Age Pop.): 2,997,007 / 4,182,975
  2006: 50.8% (Highest Office/Voting-Age Pop.): 2,161,700 / 4,257,230
  2008: 69.0% (Highest Office/Voting-Age Pop.): 2,983,417 / 4,324,620
Youth Turnout (18–29 years old)
  2000: 51%
  2002: 24%
  2004: 65%
  2006: 40%
  2008: 58%

STATEWIDE ELECTION OUTCOMES

Presidential Vote 2004: 2,997,007 votes cast
  Bush (R)   49.3%
  Kerry (D)   49.7%
Presidential Vote 2008: 2,983,417 votes cast
  Obama (D)   56.2%
  McCain (R)   42.3%
Gubernatorial Vote 2006: 2,161,700 votes cast
  Doyle (D)   52.7%
  Green (R)   45.3%
Electoral College Votes: 10

VOTING REGULATIONS

Residency Requirements: Wisconsin resident for 10 days.
Absentee Ballot: Yes
  Criteria: Available for all voters. Must be requested by 5:00 p.m. on day prior to election. Must be returned by 8:00 p.m. on day of election.

Advance Voting: Yes
   Criteria: Available as in person absentee voting requested by 5:00 p.m. on day prior to election and returned by 8:00 p.m. on day of election.
Provisional Balloting: Yes
Vote by Phone: No
Registration Deadline: 20 days prior to election by mail; day prior to election in person at municipal clerk's office; day of election in person at polls.
Secretary of State Website: http://elections.state.wi.us/

CANDIDATE REGULATIONS

Qualifications
   Governor: 18 years old, state resident (qualified elector)
   State Senator: 18 years old, district resident, state resident for 1 year
   State Representative: 18 years old, district resident, state resident for 1 year
Filing Fees
   Governor: $0
   State Senate: $0
   State House: $0
Filing Deadlines
   Presidential Primary: January 2
   Independent/Third Party in Presidential Election: September 2
   Congressional Primary: July 13, 2010
   Independent/Third Party in General Election: July 13, 2010, 5:00 p.m.
Online Filing: No
Petition Signature Requirements
   Major Party: President: 10,000
   Minor Party: President: 2,000

JUDICIAL ELECTIONS

Justice chosen: At large
Method of Selection
   Unexpired Term: Gubernatorial appointment from judicial nominating commission.
   Full Term: Nonpartisan election
No. of Judges: 7
Terms: 10 years
Method of Retention: Nonpartisan election

PRIMARY ELECTION PROCESS

Presidential
  Type: Primary/Open
  Date: February 19, 2008
State
  Type: Primary/Open
  Date: September 14, 2010

STATE CAMPAIGN FINANCE

Contribution Regulations: Contributions limits for noncandidate individuals vary according to the office involved, but calendar year contributions may not exceed $10,000. A state office candidate who receives an election campaign fund grant is limited to twice the amount an individual may contribute for the office. A state or local office candidate may not accept contributions from all political committees combined (including the election campaign fund) during a campaign of more than 65% of the candidate's authorized disbursement level or from all political committees combined (other than political party and legislative campaign committees) and the election campaign fund of more than 45% of the authorized level. Political committees are limited in the amounts that may be contributed, with the amount varying according to the office involved. Political parties may not receive contributions of more than $150,000 during any biennium from all nonparty and nonlegislative-campaign political committees or more than $6,000 from any one such committee. Corporations and association may not make nonreferendum-related contributions and disbursements, but may establish and administer a separate segregated fund.

Fundraising Limits: The authorization levels of disbursements are as follows: (1) candidate for governor—$1,078,200; (2) candidate for lieutenant governor—$323,475; (3) candidate for attorney general—$539,000; (4) candidate for Secretary of State, State Treasurer, Justice of the Supreme Court, and the State Superintendent of Public Instruction—$215,625; (5) candidate for Court of Appeals Judge—$86,250; (6) candidate for State Senator—$34,500 total in the primary and election, with disbursements not exceeding $21,575 for either the primary or the election; (7) candidate for Representative to the Assembly—$17,250 total in the primary and election, with disbursements not exceeding $10,775 for either the primary or the election; (8) candidate for Circuit Judge—$86,250; (9) in any jurisdiction or district (other than a judicial district or circuit) with a population of 500,000 or more, candidate for County Executive—$269,500, District

Attorney—$161,725, County Supervisor—$17,250, and other countywide office—$107,825; (10) in a city of 1st class, candidate for Mayor—$269,550, City Attorney—$161,725, Alderman—$17,250, and any other citywide office—$107,825; and (11) candidate for any local office who is elected from a jurisdiction or district with less than 500,000 inhabitants—an amount equal to the greater of $1,075 or 53.91% of the annual salary (rounded to the nearest $25) or 32.35 cents per inhabitant of the jurisdiction or district, but in no event more than $43,125.

Electronic Filing: No.

Reporting Cycle Dates: Reports are due 8–14 days before a primary or general election; continuing semiannual reports between January 1 and 31 and July 1 and 20 until termination report is filed.

LOBBYING GUIDELINES

Each organization employing lobbyists must pay a $375 registration fee plus $125 for each individual the organization employs as a lobbyist. Individual lobbyists in addition must have a lobbying license that requires a fee of $250 to lobby for one organization or $400 to lobby on behalf of multiple organizations. Registrations expire at the end of even numbered years.

BALLOT INITIATIVES AND REFERENDUM

Referendum: No
Ballot Initiative: No
Recall Election: Yes

WYOMING

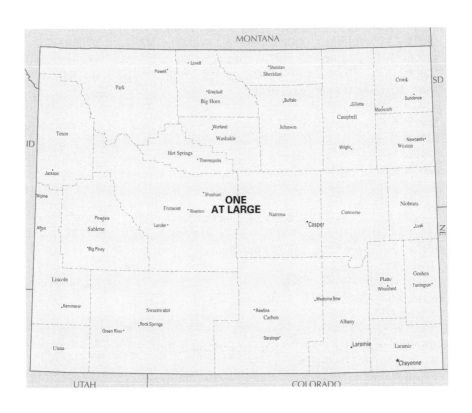

STATE VOTER TURNOUT

Population: 522,830
Registered Voters
  2000: 220,012
  2002: 241,200
  2004: 273,950
  2006: 263,083
  2008: 233,141
Turnout
  2000: 58.2% (Highest Office/Voting-Age Pop.): 213,726 / 366,055
  2002: 49.2% (Highest Office/Voting-Age Pop.): 185,459 / 373,639
  2004: 63.7% (Highest Office/Voting-Age Pop.): 243,428 / 381,868
  2006: 49.4% (Highest Office/Voting-Age Pop.): 193,892 / 392,344
  2008: 63.0% (Highest Office/Voting-Age Pop.): 256,035 / 406,460
Youth Turnout (18–29 years old)
  2000: 47%
  2002: 30%
  2004: 53%
  2006: 26%
  2008: 50%

STATEWIDE ELECTION OUTCOMES

Presidential Vote 2004: 245,789 votes cast
  Bush (R)   68.2%
  Kerry (D)   28.8%
Presidential Vote 2008: 256,035 votes cast
  Obama (D)   32.4%
  McCain (R) 64.4%
Gubernatorial Vote 2006: 193,616 votes cast
  Freudenthal (D) 70.0%
  Hunkins (R)   30.0%
Electoral College Votes: 3

VOTING REGULATIONS

Residency Requirements: Wyoming and precinct resident
Absentee Ballot: Yes
  Criteria: Available to all voters; no excuse is necessary. May be re-
quested any time throughout calendar year of election, except on day

of election. Recommended application deadline is 17 days prior to election. Must be returned by 7:00 p.m. on day of election.

Advance Voting: Yes

   Criteria: Available for all voters beginning 40 days prior to election and ending at close of business on day prior to election.

Provisional Balloting: Yes

Vote by Phone: No

Registration Deadline: 30 days prior to election or at polls on day of election.

Secretary of State Website: http://soswy.state.wy.us/Elections/Elections.aspx

CANDIDATE REGULATIONS

Qualifications

   Governor: 30 years old, state resident for 5 years

   State Senator: 25 years old, district resident for 1 year, state resident

   State Representative: 21 years old, district resident for 1 year, state resident

Filing Fees

   Governor: $200

   State Senate: $25

   State House: $25

Filing Deadlines

Presidential Primary: n/a (Republican Caucus on January 5, Democratic Caucus on March 8)

   Independent/Third Party in Presidential Election: August 25 (Independent)

   Congressional Primary: May 28, 2010

   Independent/Third Party in General Election: August 23, 2010 (Independent)

Online Filing: No

Petition Signature Requirements

   Major Party: President: 5,121 (2% of voters in last general election)

   Minor Party: President: 5,121 (2% of voters in last general election)

JUDICIAL ELECTIONS

Justice Chosen: At large

Method of Selection

   Unexpired Term: Gubernatorial appointment from judicial nominating commission.

Full Term: Gubernatorial appointment from judicial nominating commission.
No. of Judges: 5
Terms: 8 years
Method of Retention: Retention election

PRIMARY ELECTION PROCESS

Presidential
 Type: Caucus/Closed
 Date: Democrats: March 8, 2008; Republicans: January 5, 2008
State
 Type: Caucus/Closed
 Date: August 17, 2010

STATE CAMPAIGN FINANCE

Contribution Regulations: Contributions by an individual during the 2-year period are limited to $25,000. Nonpolitical organizations are prohibited from making contributions except to promote the success or defeat of an initiative or referendum petition drive or ballot proposition.
Fundraising Limits: Candidates are not limited to the amount they are allowed to raise.
Electronic Filing: No.
Reporting Cycle Dates: Reports are due within 10 days after an election for all candidates.

LOBBYING GUIDELINES

All lobbyists are required to register within 48 hours of commencing lobbying activities. If the lobbyist receives more than $500 in compensation he or she shall also pay a registration fee of $25 at time of registration. The registration fee is only $5 if less than $500 in compensation is received for lobbying services.

BALLOT INITIATIVES AND REFERENDUM

Referendum: Yes
Ballot Initiative: Yes
Recall Election: No